Table of Contents

Preface

This small volume is a tribute to Sir Herbert
Butterfield, one of England's greatest historians.
His influence has spanned the Atlantic and the separate disciplines of history, political science and
religion. The contributors to the present volume
cover a similarly broad spectrum in geographic
location and social thought. All have in the best
sense been students of Butterfield. Each owes a
moral and intellectual debt that can never be repaid.
We dedicate this volume to his life and works.

I owe deep thanks to my devoted secretary, Kate
Wiencek, who has helped me enormously in the typing
and preparation of the manuscript and to her able
colleagues, Cynthia S. Miller and Shirley Kingsbury.
No scholar could have a more agreeable and efficient
group of associates.

Kenneth W. Thompson

Preface

This small volume is a tribute to Sir Harold

J. H. Thompson

Introduction

It may seem strange to some readers that a political scientist at a public affairs center in the United States should join with British, European and American scholars to pay tribute to a great British historian. The reasons are both personal and scholarly. Herbert Butterfield has exerted a profound influence on me as a political scientist, as he has on the other contributors to this volume. Second, his writings on such historical British and European political leaders as Napoleon, George III and Lord North, provide a model for studies of public affairs in any center of learning. His forthright and uncompromising emphasis on the historical dimension of politics, on getting the story right, and on walking alongside the leading historical figures about which one is writing, trying to get inside their concerns and emotions, offers an example for political scientists and historians alike. History is past politics and history of lasting value is the best political science. Herbert Butterfield by his works has earned the enduring esteem of serious thinkers who seek to explore the history of politics whether it be the most contemporary or from an earlier era.

Contributors

Louis J. Halle is one of Europe's most distinguished diplomatic historians. Before becoming a Professor of International Politics at the Geneva Graduate Institute of International Studies, he served from 1941 to 1954 in the Department of State, completing his tenure there as a member of the Policy Planning Staff in the era of George F. Kennan, Paul H. Nitze and C. B. Marshall. His monumental study, Out of Chaos, has been praised as a 20th century classic in the philosophy of history.

Savoie Lottinville was for thirty years the Director of the University of Oklahoma Press, founding and editing three large humanities publications including the Centers of Civilization Series. He is the author of The Rhetoric of History (a book often mentioned by Sir Herbert). He edited Paul Wilhelm's, Duke of Württemberg, Travels in North America, 1822-24. He created and edited the American Exploration and Travel Series published by the University of Oklahoma Press.

Norman A. Graebner was Harmsworth Professor of American History at Oxford University in 1978-79. He is Edward R. Stettinius Professor of History at the University of Virginia and one of the world's foremost authorities on the history of the Cold War. Among his writings are Cold War Diplomacy and The Age of Global Power. His criticism of moralism in foreign policy has placed him alongside Herbert Butterfield as a scholar with a Christian orientation who has strongly opposed national self-righteousness and utopianism in foreign policy and political thought.

Michael Howard is Chichele Professor of the History of War at All Soul's College, Oxford University. He is perhaps England's foremost military historian and has been a member of the British Committee on the Theory of International Politics from its creation by Sir Herbert. He combines authority in military thought with an interest in the great philosophical and religious traditions. His contribution grows out of the Third Martin Wight Memorial Lecture, the first lecturer having been Herbert Butterfield.

Adam Watson is a well known British diplomat sometimes called "the George Kennan of the British Foreign
Office." He was a student of Herbert Butterfield and
went on to various diplomatic posts, including the first
British Ambassadorship to Castro's Cuba. He succeeded
Butterfield as Chairman of the British Committee and
is currently doing research on a major study of the
state system.

Hans J. Morgenthau has held positions as Albert A.
Michelson Distinguished Service Professor of Political
Science and Modern History at the University of Chicago;
Leonard Davis Distinguished Professor of Political Sci-
ence at City College of the City University of New York
and University Professor of Political Science at the New
School for Social Research. His Politics Among Nations:
The Struggle for Power and Peace now in its fifth edi-
tion is the classic text in international politics.
Morgenthau has written on various occasions of his close
intellectual affinity with Butterfield.

Kenneth W. Thompson is the White Burkett Miller
Professor of Government and Foreign Affairs at the
University of Virginia and was formerly Vice President
of the Rockefeller Foundation when it helped Sir Herbert
establish the British Committee. Thompson is the author
of Political Realism and the Crisis of World Politics
and Ethics, Functionalism and Power in International
Politics.

I

Butterfield as Historian

HERBERT BUTTERFIELD: THE HISTORIAN AS PHILOSOPHER

Louis J. Halle

There seems to be agreement among the historians
that they should always tell the truth, and Ranke ar-
ticulated every proper historian's ideal when he said
that history should present the past as it really was.
But the historian cannot examine the past directly, as
a zoologist examines a frog, because it is gone
forever. The object of his research does not exist.

Of course it is no more than an infinitesimal por-
tion of the vanished past that the historian tries to
recover. Only think how much happened the world around
at any given moment in the past, leaving no evidence in
our day. The historian disregards all except certain
selected categories of information for which some evidence remains, and which seem worth an attempt at reconstruction on the basis of that evidence.

"Reconstruction" and "evidence" are the key words.
The first is not to be taken literally. Holbein's
portrait of Henry VIII is both reconstruction and evidence, but it is not Henry VIII. It is merely some
variously colored matter spread on canvas to show what
he looked like. The historian can never do any better
than this, and if it is Henry VIII that he is recon-
structing he does not enjoy Holbein's advantage of actually seeing him, or ever having seen him, with his
own eyes. He has to reconstruct him in imagination.

He does so, to be sure, on the basis of evidence,
such as the evidence left by Holbein. But the evidence
is always inadequate, generally biased, and altogether
wanting, or virtually so, in respect to the most inti-
mate aspects of a human being. Imaginative reconstruc-
tions of Cleopatra generally represent her as a dark-
eyed, dark-haired Egyptian beauty. But she may have
been a blue-eyed blonde, since she was probably of
almost pure Macedonian descent (the Ptolemys having
interbred by incest since the days of Alexander), and
the Macedonians may have been fair-haired and blue-
eyed. There is no reason to believe that she had any
Egyptian blood in her at all. Moreover, her portraits
on ancient coins would lead any man of our own times
to regard her face as her misfortune.

If it is impossible to reconstruct Cleopatra's outward lineaments as they actually were, how shall the historian reconstruct what went on in her mind? Mark Antony himself must often have wondered about it--at least, so I suppose in the absence of evidence, and what evidence we have leaves no doubt that he knew her more intimately than any historian since could hope to.

Admitting how little evidence we have of Cleopatra's inner life, and even of her outer being, it is nevertheless clear that the historian does not always have to do with such paucity. Not only do we have photographs of Abraham Lincoln, and descriptions of him by eye-witnesses (although, as every trial lawyer knows, most eye-witness evidence is unreliable). Better still, he was the most articulate of men, and in such informal writings as his letters exceptionally self-revealing. In this case we can have a good idea of what the individual was like on the basis of the evidence left behind. But what we have is still only an "idea," an image developed in the historical imagination--which is basically the same imagination as that of novelist or playright.

One would think that those of us who have had to face the challenge of historical reconstruction would be the most poignantly aware of the limits and uncertainties to which I refer. But historians have their share of our common humanity, which manifests itself in the exaggerated claims we are all disposed to make for our own professions.

Is there any corruption more insidious and far-reaching than this? Every church that was ever founded, although founded for the salvation of souls, has quickly come to put its own promotion first. The run-of-the-mill historian, like the run-of-the-mill in any other academic field, wants the lay public to believe that historiography has at last developed a "methodology" that gives its findings the validity of scientific truth. (An historian's review of a recent book of mine found that the merit he saw in it was marred by certain errors, such as my assertion that the historian cannot really know what went on in Cleopatra's mind when she decided to participate in the Battle of Actium.)

Until the late nineteenth century, the historian's profession had generally been regarded as simply a branch of literature. (An example of this was provided almost cynically by Grote, who, referring to his account

2

of early Greek history, for which he had to depend so
largely on legend, wrote: "I know nothing so disheart-
ening and unrequited as the elaborate balancing of what
is called evidence concerning these shadowy times and
persons. If the reader blame me for not assisting him,
if he ask me why I do not withdraw the curtain and dis-
close the picture, I reply, in the words of the painter
Zeuxis, that the curtain is the picture.") Thucydides'
history of the Peloponnesian War, although it represented the closest approach the historian could make
to "the way it really was," belonged to the same general category as Plutarch's Lives and Shakespeare's
historical plays, even if it had less of invention.
This was art, not science, although no less honorable
for that. Then such historians as Bury at Cambridge
began to insist that historiography could be and should
be a science like geology (which also reconstructs the
past).

Even in the absence of evidence, a certain experience of human nature leads me to suspect that these
historians were influenced, however unconsciously, by
envy of the prestige that was accruing to the natural
sciences at the time. It was in science that mankind
was making its great and spectacular advances. Was it
not humanly natural, then, that those who were more
concerned for the promotion of the church than for the
salvation of souls should have wished to associate
their own profession with what was achieving such high
standing in the minds of men (not excluding those who
allocate the funds on which academic budgets are
based)? The sudden insistence that history is a science, no less than chemistry, seems to me suspect.

My suspicion requires a major qualification. It
is that the research which precedes the actual writing
of history should indeed by scientific, in the same
sense that geological research is. The evidence should
be tested, and then accepted only in so far as it is
found reliable. Neither Herodotus nor Plutarch, both
of them purely literary figures, had done this. Gibbon
may sometimes have given less attention to the testing
of his evidence than to the rhythm of his prose.
"With Macaulay," said Gooch, "truth is sometimes bar-
tered for a telling phrase or a resounding epithet."
Carlyle did not sufficiently cultivate scientific
objectivity. The movement to make history scientific--
by reference to sources, by the adoption of a critical
attitude toward them, and by the cultivation of objec-
tivity--a movement that began in nineteenth-century

3

Germany and was communicated to the Anglo-Saxon world principally by Lord Acton, would have been overdue at any time after Herodotus.

But the paucity of the evidence available to the historian remains, and over a wide area, embracing what is most inward and profound, its reliability is doubtful. After the historian has been as conscientious as you please in dealing with it, the real task, which is the formulation of conclusions in actual writing, remains. Since this depends on imagination, it is the historical imagination that has the final say.

I here put forward (albeit a bit too bluntly) the thesis that the formulation of such conclusions as count cannot be scientific in any strict sense. They are the product of the historian's understanding of human nature, his insights into human behavior. This was exemplified by a principal pioneer of scientific historiography when Acton uttered his dicta (1) that all great men are bad men, and (2) that all power corrupts. The statements may be true (if somewhat too absolute in their epigramatic sententiousness), but fundamentally they are the product of what we may call Shakespearean insight, not of scientific method or methodology. When the historian has completed his preliminary work as another Lyell, when he has completed his scientific research, he must still become another Shakespeare to do the main job.

The creative imagination comes into play when the historian has to compose in one coherent and meaningful picture the data, meaningless by themselves, that have been elicited by scientific research. "For though experience is all one piece, it comes to us in fragments and we only know it in parts, and the man who wishes to understand it and to map out its meaning, must in looking at past and present find a oneness that is not apparent in that mass of details and people and events that confront him; he must divine a synthesis."[1]

+   +   +

4

The claim that a newly developed scientific methodology has made the historian infallible, even when
it comes to reading Cleopatra's mind, is to be associated with the ten thousand ordinary workers in the
ant-heaps of Academe. By contrast, the occasional
great historian is more conscious than any layman can
be of the fallibility to which historiography is subject by the very nature of the material on which it
has to work--the limitations of its adequacy and reliability alike. He knows that what he has to reconstruct,
before all, is human nature, individual and collective.
And he has to reconstruct it, not under familiar present circumstances but under the quite different cultural and psychological circumstances of other days when
men had other attitudes from our own: (What an immense
act of imagination it takes to place oneself in an entire world one has never directly experienced!) Moreover, the great historian, necessarily having a knowledge of human nature above the ordinary, knows poignantly the pitfalls to which he and his fellow historians are exposed. He knows the inescapability of what
is bias, although it presents itself as rightness or
righteousness, and the effect of bias on the historian's
conclusions. Knowing all this, he cannot regard even
his own most devoted work as other than more or less
true, and he is bound to read the work of others with
a skepticism that, not necessarily disrespectful, is
based on the irreducible recalcitrance of what the
historian has to work with.

Having said this much, I have now, in effect,
introduced Sir Herbert Butterfield.

+   +   +

All great historians are bound to be, in one way
or another, philosophers of history, preoccupied with
significance, with meaning, with the underlying nature
of historical reality, with the insufficient validity
of historial reconstruction. This is so true of Sir
Herbert that most of his books are commentaries on the
writing of history rather than accounts of what such
writing deals with. He is the historian of historiography, who subjects the work of past historiographers
to philosophical examination. It would not be wrong,
therefore, to regard him as a philosopher--like the
Harvard philosopher, George Santayana.

5

I have always found Santayana's writings as frustrating as they are fascinating. In page after page of exquisitely subtle commentary on the nature of reality--or, rather, on the nature of our experience of what we take to be reality--he seems always just about to come to some grand conclusion that will constitute, surely, revelation itself. But he never does.

There is something of this in the works of Butterfield, albeit with a salutary difference. In his case, he shows himself always anxious to do justice to both sides of a controversy. For example, as a devout Christian he must, one supposes, regard Marxism as a manifestation of pagan blindness, but as a devout Christian he is especially determined not to be unfair. Therefore, in his essay on "Marxist History"[2] he devotes far more space to softening each criticism than to making it--so that one could wonder, at last, whether he might not believe that, erroneous as Marxist materialism must be accounted, it is still rather a good thing.

With Santayana one must learn to satisfy oneself with the beauty of the process by which he makes his way toward the missing conclusion. With Butterfield, time and again, the reward is in brief passages of such power and beauty that they constitute, time and again, something like secular revelation. I know of no other writer whose works would, by themselves, provide in such measure the material for a dictionary of golden passages. (An exception must be made for Winston Churchill, whose utterances have already constituted a dictionary of quotations,[3] and the same could surely be done, if less voluminously, in the case of Butterfield.) Let me, then, make the rest of this tribute a setting for quotation, and no more than that.

I have already commented on the inadequacy of historical evidence, and on the feat of imagination required of the historian who undertakes to see the world through the eyes of men who lived far away and long ago in circumstances basically different from his own. Listen, now, to Butterfield.

> We who cannot know our own friends,
> save in a fragmentary way and at
> occasional moments of self-revelation,
> cannot hope to read the hearts of
> half-forgotten kings.[4]

History can seldom recover a given
set of circumstances and make us
see a definite situation, a particular knot of human action at a
given place and a given time; if two
diplomatists meet in a certain room
to settle a problem, and afterwards
describe their proceedings to their
respective governments, or recall
them in memoirs, if Napoleon meets
Metternich in time of crisis at
Prague, we can recover a dim and
faulty account of the interview
from their conflicting descriptions;
and yet this is one of the most precise and clear situations that a
historian might wish to narrate.[5]

Every man who has an idea of the
woman Mary Queen of Scots, or who
can catch glimpses of what happened
at Waterloo, has added to history
something from his own imagination,
and has filled in the lines for
himself. The past as it exists for
all of us, the world of the past in
our minds, is history synthesised by
the imagination, and fixed into a
picture by something that amounts
to fiction.[6]

Behind a thousand sunsets there lies
a world where men were full of the
hunt and the anxious harvest-times,
and slept with their swords near at
hand. To them the Atlantic Ocean was
a thing to raise terror, a place for
strange story-telling; the demons
were not yet driven from the woods;
and earth was a precarious place in
which the elemental forces seemed
inexorable. It was a world of wild
mythologies, and of simple things
half-understood. It comes to us--
we "remember" it--in fragments like
this; and we try to piece it together
again. The centuries have tiptoed and
gone, and the things that people have
been afraid of, the things that have
raised a thrill, the things men have

7

talked and joked and told easy lies
about, have not always remained the
same. Their logic has been different
from our logic, as a schoolboy's is
different from a priest's. The things
which in their thinking they were
always referring to, mirrored the world
they knew. The ideas that were handy
to their minds, the words that came
soonest to their lips, the turn that
was easiest to their talk, their whole
fund of metaphors and expressions,
betrayed their preoccupations and lit
up the background of their lives.
Perhaps the Sunday church-bell sounded
differently to their ears and reached
a hidden corner in their minds. Perhaps
they had not learned to think of the
stars as loveliness. For them there
could be no evening silhouettes of
chimney-pots and telegraph-wires against
the glaring moon, no dream of long white
roads that should shake with hurried,
humming traffic--the pictures they felt
at home with were not the same as ours.
And just as, in a land where earthquakes
are to be expected, the fact must give
a twist to the art of building, the
thoughts of architects, so, in those
distant ages, the world that people
knew, the things they felt at home
with, a hundred significant details,
moulded the forms of their thoughts,
and conditioned the terms of their
thinking, and made the maps of their
minds.[7]

The historian can never quite know
men from the inside--never quite
learn of piety in a devout religious
leader. For the same reason he can
never quite carry his enquiries to
that innermost region where the
final play of motive and the point
of responsibility can be decided.
The historian fails to pierce the
most inward recesses and the essential parts of a man; and all he can
depend on is a general feeling for
human nature, based ultimately on

8

self-analysis, but further enlarged
in a general experience of life.
Much can be achieved by a constant
practice of that kind of imaginative
sympathy which works on all types
and varieties of men and acquires a
certain feeling for personality. But
the only understanding we ever reach
in history is but a refinement, more
or less subtle and sensitive, of the
difficult--and sometime deceptive--
process of imagining oneself in
another person's place.[8]

I do not personally feel that in modern times technical history, in spite
of all the skill that has gone to the
making of it, has ever been taken up
by a mind that I should call Shakespearean in its depth and scope,
save possibly in the remarkable
case of Ranke.[9]

(I allow myself to surmise that, if it had not been
for the qualification "modern," Butterfield would have
made an exception of Thucydides as well as of Ranke.)

The Delphic oracle found Socrates the wisest man
alive because he alone knew his own ignorance. Surely
the wisest historians are those who share this ultimate
knowledge. In a passage too long to quote Butterfield
maintains that all history is, in greater or lesser
degree, error; so that the task of the historian must
be to work, by constant correction, for an ever-contin-
uing reduction in the degree to which the pictures men
make of the past are erroneous.[10] In this context I
apply the following comment to those little historians
who think they can, by the mystery of their methodology,
read Cleopatra's mind.

If our Western civilisation were to
collapse even more completely than
it has done, and I were asked to
say upon which of the sins of the
world the judgment of God had come
in so signal a manner, I should
specify, as the most general of
existing evils and the most terrifying in its results, human presump-
tion and particularly intellectual

9

arrogance. There is good reason for
believing that none of the fields of
specialised knowledge is exempt from
this fault; and I know of no miracle
in the structure of the universe that
should make me think even archbishops
free of it. But it is the besetting
disease of historians, and the effect
of an historical education seems very[11]
often actually to encourage the evil.

+   +   +

In teaching World War II to a generation of students who did not experience it, what I have found
hardest is to communicate the anxiety and sometimes
the despair of those in the liberal democracies who,
in 1939 and 1940, so far from having foreknowledge of
Hitler's defeat, found reason to believe that his
power had grown to the point of invincibility. The
opposition had been too little and too late. But the
historian, if he is to reconstruct the past in terms
of psychological atmosphere and human emotion, on the
basis of which men assumed certain positions or took
certain decisions, must in imagination supress his
own hindsight and, by something like electromagnetic
induction, that of the reader.

Those of us who at the present time
are engaged in the study of some
particular period of the past have
come to be aware of the importance
of unloading our minds of all remem-
brance of after-events. For certain
purposes it is important to follow
the story of the year 1788 without
that particular bias which comes
from the fore-knowledge that the
French Revolution was to occur in
the following year. And we are
liable to fall into fallacies or
optical illusions if we judge every
step in the negotiations of July,
1914, in the light of our awareness
that they were certain to issue in
a European war by the close of the
month.[12]

10

In every field of academic learning, the revolutionary advances in knowledge or understanding have tended to be the work of men outside the academic establishments, even if in their fringes. (Darwin, who had been trained for the ministry, was not a professor of biology. Einstein, unaware of some of the principal developments in the physics of his time, was an examiner in the Swiss patent office when he worked out his Special Theory of Relativity.) The reason is, surely, that graduate study imposes an indoctrination in orthodoxy, on the basis of a distintion between what is "sound" and what is "unsound," that simply imprisons the mind. This is not something that most professors are prepared to recognize, but Professor Butterfield, in his stature, had clearly transcended the limits of his academic career when he wrote:

> It is notorious that the Scientific Revolution of the seventeenth century had to by-pass the universities and found it necessary to supplement these with new establishments of its own. And even the scientists cannot escape the constitution of things which seems to decree that teaching-bodies are more fitted to continue the globe in its existing course than to guide it into new regions of the sky.[13]

I say that Sir Herbert, who has spent his whole life in the groves of Academe, has transcended its limitations. To introduce a paradox that this entails I must here refer to my own entirely different experience. For I spent the first half of my career as a functionary in a foreign office, generally close to where decisions of policy, on which everything depended, were being made with considerable anguish of conscience. Under the constant impress of this experience over the years, I came to one simple and transcendent conclusion that seems to me at the heart of the human plight and the human tragedy. It is that the great questions for decision all arise out of what are ethical dilemmas in the literal sense of the word. They are choices among alternative evils only. This is quite different from the picture one gets from the popular press and popular commentary generally, where all choices tend to be presented in Manichean terms as choices between a good course and an evil one, even as choices between what is righteous and what is wicked.

11

Another and not unrelated impression, which became
more vivid to me with the years, was that the topmost
decision-makers, the political leaders, are beset by
such overwhelming pressures from this side or the other
that they have nothing like the scope for decision which
is popularly attributed to them. (Dean Acheson, an
exceptionally strong and a moral man, was poignantly
impressed by this in his career as the American Secretary of State.) An obvious example is that of the
irresistible popular pressure which allowed the Truman
Administration no alternative to disbanding the wartime
American Army in 1945, before peace had been made, even
though it knew that to do so was to invite disastrous
consequences, perhaps to destroy any possibility of
following the War by a true peace. But examples are
provided by virtually all basic decisions that have to
be made; because mistakes accumulate and, accumulating,
foreclose choice.

I know of no other historian who understands all
this as Butterfield does. It is as if he had lived it
all himself, although in terms of his actual career it
can represent little more than a prodigy of purely
imaginative understanding.

And now I come to what seem to me the most notable
short passages in his writings, passages that I have
quoted in print and repeatedly to my students in lecture
courses.

> Behind the great conflict of mankind
> is a terrible human predicament which
> lies at the heart of the story; and
> sooner or later the historian will
> base the very structure of his nar-
> rative upon it. Contemporaries fail
> to see the predicament or refuse to
> recognise its genuineness, so that
> our knowledge of it comes from later
> analysis--it is only with the progress
> of historical science on a particular
> subject that men come really to recog-
> nise that there was a terrible knot
> almost beyond the ingenuity of man to
> untie. It represents therefore a
> contribution that historical science
> itself has added to our interpretation
> of life--one which leads us to place
> a different construction on the whole
> human drama, since it uncovers the

12

tragic element in human conflict.
In historical perspective we learn
to be a little more sorry for both
parties than they know how to be for
one another.[14]

And again:

As regards the real world of international relations I should put forward the thesis (which, if it is true,
would seem to me to be not an unim-
portant one) that this condition of
absolute predicament or irreducible
dilemma lies in the very geometry of
human conflict. It is at the basis of
the structure of any given episode in
that conflict.[15]

The understanding represented by the two passages
I have just cited leads to an abhorence of the Pharisaism, and its associated Manicheism, so dominant in
public discussion everywhere, and to a charity that is
the logical response to a reality so terrible. Referring to the post-war conflict between East and West,
to the Cold War, Butterfield wrote:

The resulting conflict is more likely
to be hot with moral indignation--one
self-righteousness encountering an-
other--than it would have been if the
contest had lain between two hard-
headed eighteenth-century masters
of realpolitik. In such circumstances the contemporary historians on each side will tend to
follow suit, each locked in the
combative views of his own nation,
and shrieking morality of that
particular kind which springs
from self-righteousness. That is
one of the reasons why contemporary history differs so greatly
from what I have called academic
history. In all that I am saying
I am really asserting, moreover,
that the self-righteous are not
the true moralists either in
history or in life.[16]

13

A final quotation in this context.

> When it comes to the question of his-
> torical interpretation people may have
> all the evidence before them and may
> get the externals of the story correct,
> and yet may go astray by putting the
> story, so to speak, in the wrong
> universe. It is one of our optical
> illusions, for example, to imagine
> Philip II of Spain more free than
> he really was, just as we fail to
> realise how our thinking must be
> conditioned through having to be
> done under the limitations of the
> English language. We fail to see
> how Philip II was limited by his
> world and hemmed in by all kinds of
> forces and conditioning circumstances;
> and we dismiss him with facile con-
> demnation because we imagine that
> the universe in which he lived was
> freer than it really was--indeed,
> we constantly imagine that the
> range of options open to a states-
> man at a given moment is greater
> than in reality turns out to be the
> case.[17]

Butterfield's awareness of the dilemmas that confront statesmen and of the limitations on their freedom of choice logically invites compassion for one's
enemies as for one's friends. "Even if we have to
fight men," he writes, "we are not permitted to hate
them or to foresake compassion...."[18]

And now for the paradox that justified me in
invoking my own experience a few paragraphs back. It
was eye-witness experience of the agonizing limitations
under which men have to make the decisions that spell
life or death for nations that engendered in me an
abhorrence of self-righteousness and Pharisaism, and
that led me to value compassion as I do truth. If
one reads, especially, Sir Herbert's essay on "The
Christian and Historical Study"[19] one is left with the
impression that what led him to these same conclusions
was nothing of the sort. It was, rather, his acceptance of what the Bible presents as history, his belief
in the personal God who created man in his image, his
belief in the centrality of man in the universe, and

14

finally his conviction that "God is Love." To my mind, he arrives at what the direct experience of reality teaches by way of a body of belief to which I myself cannot attribute the validity of literal reality.

What I have thought worth commenting on here is the fact that the experience of human reality, by itself, and the teachings of a religion should lead to the same conclusion. This has meant that, in Sir Herbert's case, religious belief has not militated, as in so many other cases, against a perception of the nature of human reality that is not surpassed, and perhaps not equaled, by any other academic mind of our day.

Everything is brought together in Butterfield's philosophy: science and literature no less than reality and religion. Both his scientific discipline and his literary mastery are evident in the quotations I have presented. Indeed, I doubt that there is any better example in our time of the historian as scientist and as man of letters alike.

FOOTNOTES

[1] Sir Herbert Butterfield, The Historical Novel. (Cambridge, England: The University Press, 1924), 86.

[2] Butterfield, History and Human Relations. (London, England: Collins, 1951).

[3] Winston S. Churchill, Maxims and Reflections. (London, England: Eyre and Spottiswoode, 1947).

[4] The Historical Novel, op. cit., 15.

[5] Ibid., 16.

[6] Ibid., 22.

[7] Ibid., 100-102.

[8] "Moral Judgments in History," in History and Human Relations, op. cit., 116-117.

[9] "Dangers of History," in ibid., 170.

[10] See ibid., 171-173.

[11] Ibid., 169.

[12] "History as a Branch of Literature," in ibid., 246.

[13] Butterfield, Man on His Past. (Cambridge, England: University Press, 1955), 39.

[14] "The Tragic Element in Modern Conflict," in History and Human Relations, op. cit., 16-17.

[15] Ibid., 20.

[16] Ibid., 21-22.

[17]"Marxist History," in ibid., 72-73.

[18]"Christianity and Human Relations," in ibid., 47.

[19]Ibid.

SIR HERBERT BUTTERFIELD AS A NARRATIVE HISTORIAN

Savoie Lottinville

Half a century ago, a reviewer of Sir Herbert Butterfield's newly published The Peace Tactics of Napoleon, 1806-1808, suggested in the English Historical Review that the author, in treating the subject narratively and with recognizable literary skill, would not realize sufficient reward for his pains. The judgment, now obviously wide of the mark, was one commonly applied in that era, and even much later, to narrative historical works. In the United States it took the form, "If the work is readable, it can't possibly be good history." Today few students of Continental European history would analyze this signally important book in any but respectful, admiring terms. Its freshness, vigor, and reliability in the complex area of diplomatic history give it special place in the now vast historiography of the twentieth century.

There are understandable reasons for the still continuing misgivings about narrative history as a technique, even though it is the oldest of historical-- indeed literary--forms. Simply stated, it imposes upon the writer a mastery of narrative skills, quite aside from the command he may have gained over the historical problem before him. Thus the research-oriented scholar who essays a narrative development of his subject is called upon to learn a second craft, whose principles are quite as exacting as the evaluation of data and whose sequential forms will admit of no relaxation literarily. The challenge is not for everyone and the disinclination to believe it is possible has always been strong critically.

Those who doubt, however, may wish to consider the example that disproves the presumed rule. In a life- time of historical production, embracing in his per- sonal bibliography more than 125 titles--books, arti- cles, reviews, and lectures--Sir Herbert Butterfield has never been far from narrative history as the con- cept of his choice.[1] The word narrative as substantive appears often, even in his analytical and critical work, as if, in an unconscious acceptance of reality, it had

become synonymous with history itself. No long recall
of the past of man and his societies is needed to confirm the fact that this transference is correct. Re-
duced to its most recognizable terms, narrative answers the never-ceasing quest imposed by the question,
How did it happen? The painstaking skill with which
the author has reconstructed sequentially the course
of events, the critical insight he has exhibited in
reconciling, or discarding, conflicting historical
evidence, and his rejection of advocacy--all of these
are components of a more highly developed narrative
skill than perhaps any other we have witnessed in our
time.

     No historian, however, escapes the obligation to
analyze and explain. This, obviously, is the analytical genre, and on occasion, as in the striking narrative example of The Peace Tactics of Napoleon, it will
appear in Sir Herbet Butterfield's constructions. It
is necessarily central to his method in many of his
essays and reviews. For the active student of history,
old or young, its appearance, even in a long narrative
sequence, prefaced by something like, "The history of
this period cannot be understood merely..." often pro-
vides a sharply defined interpretation and a historical
maxim of much wider application than merely to the
case at hand. In this we have not only a directional
aid in the narrative pursuit of the historical problem
but the response of the teacher-scholar to his obligation to pass on to others what he himself has gained
only at the cost of immense effort.

     The diplomatic situation after Napoleon had
annihilated the Russians at Friedland (June 13, 1807)
is a case in point. The Emperor, now more fully aware
than ever of Prussia's selfishness and double-dealing,
had become malevolent. Toward King Frederick William
III he had a large measure of contempt. The peace, if
it was now to be settled with Prussia's defeated ally,
would call for a play of minds at Tilsit between the
Emperor and Czar Alexander I. It is not France or
Russia or Prussia that takes a course of action, nor
any of their regularly constituted departments of
diplomacy: it is the play of personalities, "palpable
and direct":

"There is something in the history of
diplomacy which inclines to be cold
and forbidding, and lacks the full-
blooded leap of the larger story of
human lives. Like the history of
institutions it will tend to concern
itself with the development of a
system, abstracted from its human
context; it will aspire to the
mathematical theorem. There is a
balancing of forces, and adjustment
of interests; there is much that proceeds out of the logic of a situation,
there is much that seems to come by
a kind of automatic interaction.
Sometimes, in rationalisation, one
can almost forget that human beings
are at work, with play of mind and
mood and impulse; acts will not seem
to cry out for an explanation in
personality, but will be referred to
some logic of policy. And history
will fall to her greatest tempta-
tion--hearing the tick of the clock,
but forgetting to feel the pulse."[2]

The historian who possesses literary as well as
scientific command of his materials has been something
of an anomaly since the middle 1920's. The gradual
maturing of documentary study, the increasing thrusts
towards historical revision, and the accompanying ten-
dency towards severe delimitation of subject (Sir
Herbert Butterfield calls the latter "atomisation")
have been major counterforces to the development of
sound literary expression in historical terms. Whenever a commanding figure appears, however, we can
be almost certain that his literary skills flow, in
some considerable part, from his humanistic background
and his absorption of structural techniques--sometimes
from formal study in purely literary fields, sometimes
by an almost unconscious adoption of the conventions
essential to the development of both narrative and
analysis. For Sir Herbert Butterfield, we need to be
reminded that his first achievement in book form was
The Historical Novel: An Essay (1924). His indebted-
ness to the reading required for that study appears in
a number of forms in his later essays and historio-
graphical studies. But perhaps more importantly, his
imaginative application of narrative conventions en-
countered in that seemingly remote genre becomes

apparent in his own histories. A larger lesson than
the mere mechanics of story-telling, however, appears
in his essay, "History as a Branch of Literature":

> "Over and above the things that have
> been noted on the subject of literary
> historians in general, we must take
> cognizance of the remarkable fact
> that the science of history has been
> enriched even by the achievement of
> the historical novelist. This is not
> difficult to understand, for histor-
> ical abridgements may present us with
> mere formulas sometimes, and chroni-
> clers may cheat us with unexplained
> events or with facts that seem to have
> no particular context. The histor-
> ical novelist, on the other hand, if
> he takes his work seriously at all,
> is inescapably confronted with the
> problem of seeing a former age in
> its concrete detail, and on its own
> terms, and with its proper setting."[3]

Of Sir Walter Scott he observed that, "Even if nobody
ever reads him any more he will remain significant in
the history of historical science not for the light
he throws on any age of history, but because he re-
vealed so much concerning those operations which are
possible to students of the past for the achievement
of historical-mindedness." In a far more complex historical investigation, that concerning the constitutional issues of the Crown, Parliament, and the people
in the reign of George III, Sir Herbert Butterfield
had repeated opportunities to see a former age "on
its own terms." (We shall look at the latter in a
subsequent stage of this discussion.) Meantime, what
narrative canons does the author employ, and under
what kinds of historical restraints? For our purposes,
the most obvious choice of example is that with which
we began, The Peace Tactics of Napoleon.

The narrative opening is a brilliant demonstration
of the use of crisis in what might momentarily seem a
deceptive statement of conceputalization--i.e., the
direction the book is to take:

> "The fine show of armies arrayed and
> kings in proud posture had collapsed
> in medley and muddle in the twin

battles of Jena and Auerstadt. It
littered the countryside and strove
painfully to sort itself out afresh,
as the din subsided and the smoke
cleared away. Napoleon, sprawling
upon the ground to study his maps,
fell into an undignified sleep, and
his guard took silent stand around
him. Murat, writing to his master,
apologised: 'Your Majesty will par-
don my scribble, but I am alone and
dropping from fatigue,'[4] and he who
was no weakling blundered the strokes
of his pen, as if he had been drunk.
The release of the tension of battle
liberated the worst elements in the
army. The forces of the very vic-
tors seemed endangered by indisci-
pline."[5]

The footsteps of the corps d'armée, as an observer
wrote a few days later, were accompanied by "fire,
devastation, and crimes atrocious beyond belief," the
troops despising orders and the lives of their officers
threatened. The French, rummaging baggage wagons, invited peasants to join in their luck. The Prussians,
all organization lost, rushed about blindly, "officers
and men alike, ignorant of the true direction of retreat."[6] Frederick William III of Prussia, fleeing
like his troops, barely escaped capture.[7]

On October 18, 1806, four days after the battle
of Jena, the King of Prussia, his foreign minister,
Count Haugwitz, and other counselors, met to consider
a strategy for peace, Napoleon meanwhile having given
an instant dismissal of a plea for an armistice. The
dismissal had its background in the realization by
Napoleon that, as he fought this war with Prussia,
the "corollary was the entry of the Russians into
Poland. It was a contingency he had merely divined,
but if it should occur at all, he would owe the
Prussians a grudge for it."[8] Hence, even his rejection of an armistice, as his armies continued their
lightning advance into the far reaches of Germany,
contained his first diplomatic gambit to separate
Prussia from its ally, Russia, and later to wreck
the Fourth Coalition against France on the Continent.
From this point, battles (in the sense of strategy and
tactics), even the denouement of conflict, as narrative elements, fall away in favor of the diplomatic

tactics of Napoleon in advancing his Continental System and the isolation of England, still the master of the seas.

This melding of the scene of the aftermath of battle with the beginnings of the ensuing diplomatic struggles is accomplished by the author within four pages. It is accomplished without giving away any of the surprises that are in store for the principal figures in the narrative, not even excluding Napoleon himself. It satisfies the first narrative canon, that of conceptualization; it handles consummately the second canon, that of scene; and very quickly it reaches into the third, that of characterization or portraiture, e.g., the following:

> "Frederick William himself, waiting
> for news from his minister Lucchesini
> [formerly Prussian Ambassador to Paris],
> was in one of those moods when a queer
> psychological apathy fell upon his
> repressed mind, and he would busy
> himself with odds and ends of futile
> occupations and interests, like a
> harassed man who picks at a piece of
> string. He who was 'rather the con-
> scientious drudge of state than its
> first servant,' could not bear the
> awfulness of responsibility and
> shrank from taking a decision in
> matters he knew to be so momentous.
> From his way of walking around, from
> his habit of toying with trifles,
> people said he was indifferent--that
> he might have had ten kingdoms to
> lose....Frederick William wrote a
> pitiable letter to Napoleon, ex-
> pressing his anxiety and complaining
> of delay..."9

Later, when the King had received Napoleon's now matured ideas for a cessation of hostilities, he found
the terms "much more exacting than he had anticipated.
He had thought of a speedy forgiveness and then reconciliation, and a return to the fold." From this he
moved to an appeal for much more favorable terms.

The portrait of the Prussian King builds as the
narrative progresses, but from this initial narrative
sketch we have two keys to a figure who is major in

the diplomatic events of the years 1806 and 1807:   he
was himself weak, whining, and forever seeking by
strategems to preserve his old boundaries; and he was
always directed in his courses by ministers far abler
at chess than he could ever be.

Portraiture, as a matter of fact, must be at a
premium in a narrative that contains Napoleon Bonaparte
as its pivotal figure. The enormous range of his en-
ergies, his discernment of others' diplomatic objectives, his skill in checkmating even the best conceived
moves of his opponents, and his insistence on direct
personal involvement in most of the affairs of state--
all of these characteristics invited--rather demanded--
adequate personal foils for his genuis. It is less
the quality of his figure or his presence than the
quality of his thinking that arrests the author and
intrigues us. For example:

Having first declined to offer an armistice to
Prussia after Jena, Napoleon entertained a plan for
a restoration of peace, soon abandoned that idea in
favor of an armistice which would make of Prussia a
hostage until further Continental conquests (which he
threatened) had convinced Europe of the need for a
general peace settlement. There would be no separate
peace with Prussia. "To end the French occupation,
the Prussians would set everything in motion for the
cessation of the war."[10] Thus the Emperor had thrown
Prussia back into the coalition which, after abject
defeat, she was attempting to escape. (That Frederick
William rejected the proposed terms of the armistice
finally offered was perhaps less the consequence of a
note which Napoleon attached to the armistice, com-
miting Prussia to join hostilities at the side of
France, than to the fact that Russian troops were
already advancing in Poland.) "Everything," says
the author, in further characterization of the
Emperor's habits of mind, "was comprehended in one
trenchant principle of policy, for Napoleon had a
way of fusing his problems together and resolving them
at a stroke, covering the whole political situation by
an imaginative leap, a bold synthesis."[11]

Was he wholly preoccupied with a scheme for peace
in the closing weeks of 1806? Not at all. The dimensions of his character would not then, or perhaps
ever, permit that.

"He was a military leader and we see
him organising armies, calling up
recruits, disposing his forces,
ordering shoes for his soldiers,
arranging the construction of
bakeries, busying himself with
all the paraphernalia of war. He
was a human mortal, and we hear of
him enjoying the balls and the
brilliant life of Warsaw, adoring
the beauty of the Polish ladies,
laying siege to the heart of the
Countess Walewska, and writing to
the Empress to reassure her about
his health, or to calm her jeal-
ousies or to prevent her from
appearing inconveniently in Poland.
He was the Emperor, ruling France
from a distance, organising propaganda, directing theatres and
newspapers, rebuking his chief of
police, aiding necessitous manu-
factures in France, and writing
'M. de Champagny, literature ought
to be encouraged'."12

Napoleon's foils, as they appear in the author's
narrative, are integral with the diplomatic developments to which the Emperor was central. But they are
not ordinary, in the sense of this historian's management of them: Lucchesini, earlier abominable to
Napoleon when he represented Prussia in Paris; the
always ambitious Talleyrand, from Napoleon's own stable
of diplomats; Baren Hardenberg, negotiating for a
Prussia in diplomatic extremis, sly master of complex
schemes and stratagems; the Czar Alexander I of Russia,
a romanticist in war-talk with his ally King Frederick
William, and a disciple easily won by Napoleon after
his defeat at Friedland; The Russian Chancellor, Baron
Budberg, more a realist at Tilsit than his Czar; Charles
James Fox, the English Foreign Secretary, who proved
himself not quite fathomable to Napoleon; and George
Canning, a far more energetic minister than those who
had preceded him; the Austrian Chancellor Count Stadion,
apostle of the general mediation in Europe for peace;
and many more. We are here reminded of Sir Herbert
Butterfield's earlier cited insistence upon the "full-
bodied leap of the larger story of human lives" in
the history of diplomacy. And through it all must run
the most intriguing of narrative illusions, the illusion of immediacy.

26

The creation of this illusion, this conviction
of immediacy on the part of the reader, is an essential function in the canons of narration, brought to
its highest development in the play and hardly less
so in the novel. To achieve it in historical writing
requires of the historian genuine powers of imaginative
presentation. For it offends credibility: we already
know what happened, if we have any general historical
knowledge at all. But in this we forget that Sir
Herbert Butterfield's historical characters do not know
what is going to happen to them. In time the author's
skill in following them arouses in us the conviction
that we had never really known either. This is the
most essential feature of the narrative canon of
continuity, with its accompanying device of suspense.
At heart it treats chronology as unfolding rather than
as past time. We look forward not backward, half convinced that the author has found sources hidden to us,
painting a historical picture quite unknown to a profession noted for its skepticism.

Narration, as the author strikingly demonstrates,
has other, even subtler nuances, e.g., the historical
question, offered the reader as unself-consciously as
if the author had no ready answer for it and is invit-
ing the reader's participation in the search for a solution. It is an aspect of immediacy, notable for its
employment at almost the same time in an account of the
Duke of Wellington and Waterloo by the author's French
counterpart, Élie Halévy.[13] Our involvement sometimes
becomes even more personal and pressing from the author's use of the impersonal pronoun you, as in the
tableau of life at the Prussian court at Memel, its
principals surrounded, sometimes comforted, by representatives of the foreign diplomatic corps:

> There was Lord Gower, 'a handsome mi-
> nor', who played the gallant to Count-
> ess Voss and gave her 'twelve pairs of
> beautiful English silk stockings'.
> There was Sir Robert Wilson, a stagey
> but irrepressible figure, a man full of
> excitement, passing on his enthusiasm
> to all around. He would give the Queen
> a copy of his book on Egypt, and send
> wine and tea to the Countess Voss; he
> would play charming chevalier to them
> both; but he would desert them at times,
> for he was in love with the bright eyes
> of danger and you could not hold him if

27

there were hope of a battle. Lord
Hutchinson was the head of the party,
but he had an unpleasant way with him,
and he was a shaggy-looking creature.
He would talk of the greatness of
Napoleon, and pooh-pooh the hopes of
victory, and shake his head in an
unbelieving way if the Russians sent
good news. So the clock beat out the
solemn days. You could laugh when the
sun was shining, but it was a pathetic
kind of laughing. You toyed with triv-
ialities and made yourself a world of
little things; it was a mere flight
from the big inescapable preoccupation.
You would make jest over a tea-cup with
the Countess Voss; only she, when she
found herself alone, would turn aside
to her diary, and write with vagrant
touches of sadness. The whole was a
kind of stage-play, as though one
danced on the edge of the abyss. And
the King--for his part, he would not
dance: he had no escape from the burden of things. You looked on him with
a sort of pity, awkward, unattractive
as he was... ."14

This last is a technique reserved to those who are very
sure of their sources and are capable, at the same
time, of managing them with an unobjectionable sensitivity which reaches out for the truth of a distant
reality. It requires only Goethe's "eine Phantasie fur
die Wahrheit des Realen."

It has been said that literary dissection almost
always destroys live specimens. Despite this risk,
there are two other aspects of the author's work in
The Peace Tactics of Napoleon which need to be noted:
his transitions and his hard-core historical sources.
Any piece of historical construction demands a considerable degree of organic unity. If it is narrative
in character and by the nature of its development must
shift from place to place and from concept to concept,
its transitional requirements are magnified--in the
interest of preserving the desired unity of presentation. Here the author's focus upon the principles and
policies of nations allied and at war affords a strong
bridge--from a defeated Prussia to the court of Russia;
from the Austrian court at Vienna to the Foreign Office

in London (for England to disgorge her acquisition of
France's conquered colonies in the West Indies in the
interest of Prussia and Continental peace); from Napoleon to the Austrian court (to prevent at all cost the
emergence of an Austrian enemy at his back as he pursued his war with Russia); from the Austrian court to
Napoleon (to mediate a general peace settlement in
furtherance of its own security); from the Prussian
court at Memel (to turn its utter dispossession by
France into a complete restoration); Prussia and Russia
at Bartenstein (April 23, 1807), agreeing on the goal
of freeing Prussia and jointly creating a barrier to
French expansion; Napoleon to the King of Prussia,
agreeing to a general congress at Copenhagen for the
restoration of peace, the Austrian mediation having
failed; the rich blend of disaster at Friedland in mid-
June, 1807, followed by diplomatic disarray in the Continental capitals and London; at Tilsit, a sudden re-
alingment of Czar Alexander to the side of Napoleon
("the men who led the Russians had a kind of startling
discontinuity in their souls, and one must be prepared
for self-contradiction and sudden rifts within a single
personality"), July 7, 1807; the isolation of England
now being completed, Napoleon's Continental System is
shaped and solidified, the Russians, in power matters,
looking eastward, the French to the western European
heartland.

The secret of the author's control over the narrative of diplomatic and political developments in these
widely separated theatres lies, I think, in his ability
to concentrate on interactions. Hence the almost undetected quality of his transitions. Even occasional
disjunctions in chronology seem to fade away in the
great blend of military consequences and diplomatic
moves and counter-moves.

The restraints upon this--or any--kind of narration are imposed by the character and relative abun-
dance or scarcity of documentary evidence. The author
reminds us that "Occasional scraps of conversations at
Tilsit come to us on a puff of wind; but lost from
their larger context they may lure us on a false trail."
Further, "Perhaps, there will always be people to argue that at Tilsit it was Napoleon who was the dupe,
and Alexander the grand deceiver; and in discussing
such a matter, it is a mistake to dogmatise too heavi-
ly."[15] For there is evidence both ways. Fortunately,
by 1929, when the author was publishing his account,
the published documents were an abundant assemblage:

29

for Prussia, Russia, Britain, France, and Austria.
Documents in the British Foreign Office were by now
open to examination by scholars. And diaries, memoirs,
memoranda, and editions of the private and public
correspondence of many of the principals were freely
available. In consequence of this, the author was
able to bring his evidence directly to bear in quotations from such scores, noting conflicting interpretations when necessary, and resolving particular historical problems. In sum, what we have before us is
the product of hard-core historical sources, examined
critically and in the spirit which the author was
later to develop in "Narrative History and the Spade-
Work Behind It."16

     Such, by way of mere rhetorical analysis, is the
story of The Peace Tactics of Napoleon. In the ensuing
forty years, Sir Herbert Butterfield's historical learning ranged from England in the eighteenth century to
Renaissance science, to the characters of Machiavelli
and Napoleon, to the essential requirements for the
study of modern history, to religion, dictatorship,
and historical bibliography and historiography. The
dilemma of making a further choice for analysis of his
methods is plain. But to an already great writing
achievement he added in 1949 George III, Lord North,
and the People, 1779-80, without which no student of
history can hope to come away with a balanced understanding of political and constitutional developments
in the age of George III. It was preceded by the
author's The Whig Interpretation of History in 1931
and followed by his George III and the Historians in
1957. It is safe to say that upon these three works
the author's great reputation in the field of English
history rests.

     In the first of these studies, he tell us what,
in actuality, his method is: "To see more than George
III could see in the minds of his opponents--to know
more than politicians consent to learn the thinking of
their political enemies--and to discern those deeper
movement which the actors in the story fail to take
account of, but which come like the beat of an ocean-
wave to deflect and over-ride their purposes--these are
the reasons why we study history."17 If this is the
reward for those who pursue history, and by implica-
tion the partial design, at least, of the historian's
efforts, from precisely which procedural habits does
the historian at work gain his ends?

For the crisis years in the reign of George III,
1779-80--as well as earlier and later--Sir Herbert
Butterfield identifies the reason for some of the
errors and confusions which have been given us in the
past: "Historical research always uncovers a multi-
plicity of complications, a forest of intricate details,
a host of qualifying facts and factors; but amongst
these we must keep our heads, and over them it is
necessary to exercise a presiding mind." If the historian does not gain control of his data, he may find
(as many have found in recent decades) that a narrative has no framework. Essentially, the risk is that
"We are denying that amongst the data before us there
is anything that give shape and cohesion to the story,
any sign that in George III and in other people there
are profounder purposes, deeper continuities of aim
and endeavour." Further, "By having a regard for the
framework of ideas and conscious purposes which George
III and everybody else possesses, the narrative acquires shape, acquires continuities. The historian
is at least left with something meaningful to inter-
pret."18

The author's thrust in the three works centering
in the reign of George III is unmistakably directed
towards an intensive search for and critical examination of the historical data underlying the period. It
complements in George III, Lord North and the People
the great narrative skills the author had exhibited
from the earliest years of his career. But the method
adds a still deeper dimension--a procedural exegis of
old, sometimes hitherto undetected, sometimes ne-
gelected, texts of source materials. Although it
rarely appears in the narrative, it works from bases
much more thoroughgoing than the well-known tests of
plausibility and consistency, and comparative authen-
tication. It is not enough to say that the author's
insistence is upon the intellectual aspect of the
historical synthesis (which can fall into simple methodology). It is much truer to say that his faith lies
in the historical spirit, guided primarily by a mind
which intends to penetrate often confusing details for
human patterns and purposes and ideas.

The year 1779 was the twentieth in the reign of
George III and the tenth in the administration of
Lord North as first minister. The King, who had insisted from the beginning of his reign on the right
of the crown to choose its own ministers and to take
an active part in the affairs of state, was now in

31

the awkward position of witnessing a war with his American colonies which was going badly, the beginnings of a war alliance between France and Spain against England, an Irish dependency in deep economic distress, and a lack of military preparedness at home which was little short of appalling. The English navy, desperately in disarray, in considerable part because of the incompetence of the First Lord of the Admiralty, Lord Sandwich, offered no sure command of the approaches to the English coast, much less those of Ireland.

Lord North, beleagured by William Eden, recently returned from a mission to North America, and the Attorney General Alexander Wedderburn for the dismissal of Sandwich and Lord George Germain, Secretary of State for the American colonies, was now overburdened with affairs of state and speaking, as he had often done before, of retirement. The complications of North's position were by March, 1779, further increased by the complexion of the King's closet, centered in North's own spoilsman, John Robinson, the Secretary of the Treasury, in close liaison with Charles Jenkinson, the Secretary of War, whom Horace Walpole described as "the sole confidant of the King." In the ministry, the vacancy in the position of a Secretary of State created by the death of the Earl of Suffolk, threw additional burdens upon Viscount Weymouth, the Second Secretary, who at best was indifferent to the ministry and less than mildly energetic.

North himself had been kept in office by a much earlier commitment (indeed a promise, apparently as legally binding as a contract) to the King to remain in his service, in spite of his miseries and his incapacities, the latter known even to himself. His depressions and inability to act with any degree of promptness and decisiveness suggested a psychological condition bordering at times on paranoia. But he was part of the King's system and the King chose to keep him rather than to find another first minister, perhaps only to see his kingdom slip back into that administration by Whig connection which had preceded his reign. The Rockinghamites were ever waiting. One of the historical penalties for George III in this is that, from North's indolence and lack of administrative command, the King achieved undeserved credit for features of his system which he had never envisaged. But from such bases, the larger fates in English political and constitutional life were pressing with astonishing speed.

32

From mid-June the near certainty of an attempted invasion of Britain or Ireland by the combination of France and Spain evoked frenzied marshalling of volunteer military companies in both island. By mid-August, the combined enemy fleet was in the Channel, but Admiral Sir Charles Hardy not only did not engage it but, sailing from the west, shuttled his fleet into Spithead on September 3. By mid-September, harassed by gales and ridden by disease, the combined enemy fleet gave up the project of a second Armada.

What followed in train domestically is the larger narrative of George III, Lord North, and the People, 1779-80. No narrative condensation or excerpting is called for here. We can only suggest what a "presiding mind" chose to do with the enormous burden of his data--and, as we may know, with wisdom and brilliance.

Sir Herbert chose, first of all, a narrative method, to discover for us "how it happened." The proportions of the task became clear when we realize that he must, for these two years, call into play the political and administrative aspects of the North ministry; the day-to-day tactics of the opposition; the role of the King and his interactions with the ministry, as well as the opponents of his administration; and the working of three well-defined movements: the near revolutionary crisis in Ireland after the Franco-Spanish threat of invasion had failed, connected with the emergence of the Irish Volunteers in a new and larger role; the Yorkshire Association, "the effective cradling of the programme of parliamentary reform--the first presentation of this issue on a genuinely national scale"; and, finally, the parliamentary opposition movement which took its initial stimulus from Edmund Burke's plea for "economical reform," but culminating dramatically in the House of Commons on April 6, 1780, in John Dunning's resolution that "the influence of the crown has increased, is increasing, and ought to be diminished."

For all of these developments, with their intensity of political conflict--often the bitterness of personal contest--we can quickly detect two features of the historical spirit at work: the still vital operation of the principle of seeing a former age "in its concrete detail, on its own terms, and with its proper setting"; and the conviction on the author's part that, even in extreme cases, the confrontation of a wrong-headed program or policy with a just opposition, whatever the immediate outcome, brings immediate and long-term gains. A society without such confrontation is likely to be of measureless mediocrity.

I wrote earlier of the author's "procedural exegesis" of documents. There is perhaps no better example than his detection that Lord North's obligation to continue in the King's service until he was relieved had the force of a legal contract. We may never know its context, but North asked the Lord Chancellor, Edward Thurlow, to secure an interpretation of it which, in time, might have permitted him to accept a Chief Judgeship.[19]

History, in some senses, writes itself, provided it has the mediative skill of a great historian. The effectiveness with which Sir Herbert Butterfield introduces quotations from appropriate sources gives us, once more, the sights and sounds and strivings of another age "on its own terms." He utilizes longer extracts from documents as well, so arranged that we read into them without a halt in most cases.

This latter technique has a special value for the attainment of the author's expressed aims when he approached the writing of George III, Lord North, and the People. "I have tried," he wrote, "not only to look at that unfortunate ministry [of Lord North] from the inside, but also to see how the Rockingham and Shelburne whigs appeared in the eyes of the administration and the closet. Without neglecting the noble picture that seems to emerge when we read of the Rockinghamites in the speeches of Burke and Fox, I have paid attention not only to the picture which they presented to George III, but also to the way in which they appeared to Christoper Wyvill and other more radical leaders. In all cases it is necessary to put the evidence of friends..."[20]

In my copy of this distinguished volume there are small slips of paper to enable me to turn quickly to crests discovered long ago in first reading. One of these falls at pages 287-90 and reads, "The descriptions of county and town meetings in the Yorkshire movement reach quite to the heart of political and social stratifications--and the lack of skill in even the most earnest of the county reformers (Wyvill) against politically skilled manipulators like Rockingham." Another appears at page 318: "Masterful handling here and elsewhere of indirect discourse in presenting public debates."

34

And in my copy of <u>George III and the Historians</u>
is a slip of paper quite as earnest, at page 206,
careting the author: "...we must have a political
history that is set out in narrative form--an account
of adult human beings, taking a hand in their fates
and fortunes, pulling the story in the direction
they want to carry it, and making decisions of their
own. We must have the kind of story in which (no
matter how much we know about the structure of politics and the conditions of the time) we can never
quite guess, at any given moment, what is going to
happen next."

FOOTNOTES

[1] R.W.K. Hinton, "Bibliography of Sir Herbert Butterfield's Writings (to 1968,)" in The Diversity of History: Essays in Honour of Sir Herbert Butterfield, edited by J.H. Elliott and H. G. Koenigsberger. (Ithaca, New York: Cornell University Press, 1970), 317-325.

[2] Sir Herbert Butterfield, The Peace Tactics of Napoleon, 1806-1808. (Cambridge, England: University Press, 1929), 231-232.

[3] Butterfield, History and Human Relations. (New York: The Macmillan Company, 1952), 243.

[4] Lettres et documents pour servir à l'histoire de Joachim Murat, IV (1910), 391. Here taken from Butterfield's internal note 1.

[5] Butterfield, Peace Tactics of Napoleon, 3.

[6] Ibid., 3.

[7] Ibid., 4.

[8] Ibid., 8.

[9] Ibid., 10-11.

[10] Ibid., 25.

[11] Ibid., 26.

[12] Ibid., 48.

[13] R.B. McCallum, Introduction to Élie Halévy, England in 1815, translated by E.I. Watkin and D.A. Barker. (New York: Peter Smith, 1949), viii-ix.

[14] Butterfield, Peace Tactics of Napoleon, 70.

[15] Ibid., 271,

[16] Butterfield, "Narrative History and the Spade-Work Behind It," History, 53.

[17] Butterfield, George III, Lord North, and the People, 1779-80. (London: G. Bell and Son, Ltd., 1948), 8.

[18] Butterfield, George III and the Historians. (London: Collins, 1957), 298.

[19] Butterfield, George III, Lord North and the People, 1779-80, 18-19.

[20] Ibid., vii.

II

Butterfield and International Politics

BUTTERFIELD AND THE THEORY
OF INTERNATIONAL POLITICS

Kenneth W. Thompson

Herbert Butterfield was born into a devout Methodist family on October 7, 1900, in Oxenhope, an in-
dustrial revolution village with 2,000 inhabitants at
the edge of the moors and a few miles from the Lanca-
shire-Yorkshire border. His father left school at ten
to work as a wool-sorter in the mill, but through self-
education trained himself to become a bookkeeper. He
carried with him through life his frustrated ambition
to have been a Methodist minister, and without pressing
his son unduly, made it clear that he would like him
to move in the same direction. It was partly in the
knowledge of the pleasure it would give his father
that Butterfield, from the age of 16 became a lay
preacher, a step which provoked the impatience of the
man who was his most stimulating teacher at the local
grammar school, a man very outspoken in his hostility
to Christianity. Later, when Butterfield was at
Cambridge University working under the famous historian, Harold Temperley, his growing interest in history,
and his consciousness of being too shy to succeed in
pastoral work, helped to draw him away from the idea
of going into the ministry. But whereas religious
and political thinkers have characteristically rebelled
against the tenets of their childhood, Butterfield has
never wavered from a fundamental Augustinian theology
that included belief in the infinite worth of human
personality, the reality of sin, the sovereignty of
God, the limitations of human nature and the fragmen-
tary character of human existence. He never espoused
Marxism, as did Reinhold Niebuhr and Paul Tillich,
two philosophers and theologians with whom he had some
affinity. He studied Marxist thought, however, and
extracted from it certain insights on conflict in
history and the importance of economic and social factors in history. A threefold interest in European and
British history, in the relations of Christianity to
history and in the theory of international relations
determined the focal points of his thought.

But for the formative influence of his childhood
and family life, Butterfield might have remained

content with traditional historical scholarship expected from a professor of modern history at Cambridge and
the editor of the Cambridge Historical Journal. He
was educated at Cambridge where he earned the degrees
of master of arts and doctor of literature. In 1923,
he became a fellow of Peterhouse at that university;
and then, in 1955 its master. He served as president
of the Historical Association of England in the late
1960's and, as a historian, was invited to take up
residence at the Institute for Advanced Study at
Princeton University. His first publication, The
Historical Novel (1924),[1] reflected his early concern
with the relation between literature and history. He
demonstrated the role of literary imagination in
furthering the actual rediscovery of the past. It
was an anachronism, he believed, to assume that the
events from another era could be understood in the
context of the present or recent past. Shorter and
more concentrated books in which the historian drew
on literary if not poetical skills might help recreate
the past and this became the standard for almost all
Butterfield's writing. He followed his first book with
a detailed study, The Peace Tactics of Napoleon, 1806-
1808 (1929),[2] an analysis of the relation between
military and diplomatic tactics of the period, including the Treaty of Tilsit in 1807. Reviewers praised
his historical portraiture and observed that he had
disproved the claims of German historians that Czar
Alexander of Russia had conspired to desert Britain;
it was the Prussians who persuaded the Czar to meet
with Napoleon on a raft in the River Nieman. He edited Select Documents of European History, 1715-1920
(1931a),[3] and began research on what was to be a lifelong interest in George III, eventuating in his George
III, Lord North and the People, 1779-1780 (1949a)[4] and
George III and the Historians (1957).[5] His intention
to write the definitive work on Charles James Fox and
George III was sacrificed to a new set of interests in
analytical historical studies which dominated his
research for the next four decades.

The first clear evidence that Butterfield was to
go beyond traditional historical research came in 1931
with the publication of The Whig Interpretation of History,[6] a critical analysis of the Whig and liberal view
of inevitable progress in history. His concern for
historiography was clearly demonstrated in this study,
which earned for him a reputation as an authentic historical genius. Although the book criticized liberal
politics and historical Protestantism, Butterfield

questioned in a more fundamental way the failure of
historians to do justice to the unique conditions and
mentality of bygone ages. It was evident in this work
that Butterfield was to follow in the steps of J.E.E.D.
Acton (even though he was a chief object of Butterfield's criticism) and Leopold von Ranke, and not that
of traditional British historians who concentrated on
what was primarily descriptive history. His subsequent
works, Napoleon (1939),[7] The Englishman and His History (1944),[8] and The Statecraft of Machiavelli (1940)[9]
carried him even further along the path of the philosopher of history and the political theorist.

In the late 1930's and 1940's, Butterfield, whose
eminence as a leading British historian was by then
unquestioned, entered a second phase of historical
writing that was inspired by the world crisis. In
1939, he lectured at four German universities on the
"History of Historiography," emphasizing the developments in the sixteenth and seventeenth centuries. He
argued that it was the Whig historians whom he criticized not the Whig politicians who had fostered freedom and moderation from the later years of Charles II.
The lectures enabled him to say that although he still
regarded the Whig interpretation as fallacious, he
believed it had helped in the development of liberty
in England. It was Whig historians who had perverted
the story and not politicians who used political compromise and political persuasion rather than coercion
and force.

In 1948, he turned to religion and history and
delivered a series of seven lectures at the request of
the Divinity Faculty of the University of Cambridge.
He expanded these lectures into six broadcasts presented in April and May 1949 by the British Broad-
casting Corporation. He amplified the major themes
of these lectures into a book entitled Christianity
and History (1949c).[10] Butterfield had hesitated to
undertake these lectures because he doubted a layman
was qualified to prepare them, and he knew the suspicion that such an enterprise could generate among his
fellow historians. But it became difficult for him to
avoid the invitation when the representatives of the
Divinity Faculty made it clear that they did not feel
that it would be most useful to have a clergyman--the
undergraduates might be more ready to listen to a man
who had made his name as a historian. His turn to
philosophical questions was doubtless inspired by the

dual crisis confronting the West: the formidable
challenge of the Soviet Union with its Marxist creed
and the position of the Western countries as "fright-
ened defenders of the status quo, upholding the values
of an ancient civilisation against the encroachments of
something new..."11 Butterfield warned that the idol-
atrous worship of some superperson, "society," "state,"
or other large-scale organization could so transform-
ing man's perspective that he would see the world as
comparable to the world of the ants. It was dangerous
to bypass history or to imagine that the natural sciences could safely be left to shape human destiny. It
was not enough to look for God or man in nature or to
conclude with Hitler in Mein Kampf that since nature is
concerned not with individual human lives but with the
development of the species, history inevitably imposes
its cruelties, idolatries, and human sacrifices. This
attitude Butterfield described as "the facile heresy
of the self-educated in a scientific age" and coun-
seled: "Too easily we may think of man as merely the
last of the animals and in this way arrive at verdicts
which we are tempted to transpose into the world of
human relations."12 Christianity and History reas-
serted the author's profound belief in the central
place of human personality in the historical process.
He protested against the opposing view of certain
behavioral social scientists and naturalists that history is the story of great collectivities to be studied
through science and mathematics as no more than another
chapter in "the great book of biology."

        Butterfield elaborated and extended this criti-
cism and restated the Christian perspective in a succession of writings in which he claimed to speak not
as a theologian but, as had Arnold J. Toynbee, as a
historian. He wrote as an individual scholar, not
interacting with other historians and theologians who
propounded an elaborate historical scheme as had
Arnold J. Toynbee. His aim, as he conceived it, was
to challenge Christians and non-Christians alike to
renew awareness of the place in history of the Christian view. He added books on Christianity in European
History (1951a);13 History and Human Relations
(1951b);14 and Christianity, Diplomacy and War
(1953).15 Whatever the questions critics have raised
about his Christian perspective, Butterfield has
resolutely maintained that history seen in its broad-
est dimensions is consonant with a Christian view of
history. He has inveighed against mere "technical
history" which falls short of a subtle comprehension

of the past. For him history at its core is a drama,
oftentimes tragic in dimension, of human personalities.
The tenets of historical scholarship require the historian to practice intellectual humility and flexibil-
ity of mind. He must walk alongside the actors in
history, placing himself in their position, seeking to
recapture their perceptions of events and to understand the problems with which they had to cope.

Another facet of Butterfield's contribution stems
from his study of science. Beginning in 1931, he had
lectured to Cambridge undergraduates on modern history
from 1492 with attention to such larger developments
and long-term movements as the Renaissance, the French
Revolution, and their interconnections. His approach,
which followed the example of Lord Acton was intended
as a reaction against the overspecialization that had
come to dominate the university study of modern history
with its use of "outlines" and dry textbook accounts
of the external relations of states. Instead he fo-
cused on the emergence and major developments of the
modern world and modern thought, devoting, for example,
approximately six lectures to the rise of modern science. These lectures brought him into contact with
prominent Cambridge scientists such as Joseph Needham
and the group at the Cavendish Laboratory, which was
in search of an ally among historians. Under the influence of these people, a history of science committee
was appointed in 1947, and it was this body which,
after a considerable conflict, induced Butterfield to
deliver in the Michaelmas term 1948 a course of lectures on the subject. The lectures led to the publication of his most successful book, The Origins of
Modern Science (1949b),[16] and to a reawakening of interest in the subject in England and America. It
brought trained scientists into touch with serious
historical study and helped produce a new generation of
historians of science.

In 1953, Butterfield was asked to deliver the
Wiles Trust lectures at Queens University, Belfast,
and he chose to return to the topic of "History of
Historiography" in the eighteenth and nineteenth centuries. The subject had been a preoccupation of German
historians and a few American historians, but despite
the efforts of Acton and his disciple, G.P. Gooch, who
wrote, History and Historians in the Nineteenth Century
(1913), it had not taken root in England. The Wiles
lectureship brought together Butterfield, who lectured
on Man on His Past (1955),[17] and ten European and

45

British historians who, as authorities on differing
aspects of his subject, criticized and commented on his
presentation. When published in 1955, these lectures
led to a considerable reawakening of interest in historiography among university undergraduates, research
students and professors. Subsequently, he wondered if
enthusiasm for historiography had gone too far and
urged that universities limit its study to historians
who were equipped by temperament and experience for
the task. Although he was pleased he had been able to
advance the work of Acton and Gooch, he believed that
for the ordinary research student, training in the
processing of evidence and the main techniques of
research must come first.

Ten years later in 1965 and 1966, he was called
on to deliver the famed Gifford lectures at the University of Glasgow, a series in which Americans such
as William James, John Dewey and Reinhold Niebuhr had
participated. Butterfield chose to address the broad
question of how the human race had come to possess a
concept of "the Past," and how and why mankind had been
interested in its past before historical writing had
begun. He speculated that early religion might have
had some influence, but wondered if it might also have
been the enemy of genuine history. The historical
mentality, he concluded, had gradually emerged from
the conflicting desire to reconcile both religious and
secular history. He believed that conclusions based
on recent research in Mesopotamian and Jewish languages
was adaptable to the kind of questions that Western
historians characteristically studied. The lectures
constituted his boldest historical adventure, for he
undertook to survey the entire "History of Historiography." His effort inspired interest, particularly
in the United States, but left him uncertain as to
whether he had or could ever acquire the universal
knowledge on which a published treatise on the subject
should be based. Then in the mid-1960's the focus of
Butterfield's interest shifted and he never returned
in a systematic way to the theme of his Gifford Lectures.

In all his historical writings, he has argued that
at one level, historical interpretation calls for
painstaking research and the ability to relive "the
lost life of yesterday" using the accumulated traces of
history "to recapture a bygone age and turn it into
something that is at once a picture and a story."[18]
In pursuit of this goal, Butterfield was following
the tradition he had absorbed from his teacher, the

master historian of diplomacy, Harold Temperley, seeking always to write history of a high and complicated texture. At another level, the historian has the obligation to identify with his subject in order neither to praise nor blame him, but, rather, to understand the circumstances confronting him. In studying the diplomatic interchanges that accompanied Napoleon's campaigns against the Fourth Coalition, Butterfield felt compelled to consult major archives in London, Paris and Vienna, the correspondence drawn from the Prussian and Russian archives, and the reports of ambassadors, ministers, and spies to the leading statesmen of that day. His purpose was to mirror the thoughts of the major personages of the time and to uncover "...the strange tangle, the hidden undercurrents and the clash of personalities that lay behind a Napoleonic war."[19] Even in the two studies of Napoleon written early in his career, the structure of Butterfield's maturing view of history was discernible. The unfolding story was for him unpredictable and wayward, based on the interaction of diverse personalities proceeding, not in accordance with predetermined doctrines of a superior people or of inevitable progress, or with consequences clearly linked to their intentions, but with goals and actions whose efforts are deflected by the mysterious workings of Providence.

Butterfield's essential ideas about historical studies matured and were well-defined before he was 31 years of age. He had won the LeBas Prize at Cambridge for his first book, The Historical Novel but his third, The Whig Interpretation of History (1931b), lay the foundations of all his later works with their underlying theme of "...the complexity of human change and the unpredictable character of the ultimate consequences of any given act or decision of men."[20] Historical writing must communicates the texture of such complexity. Historical change for Butterfield necessitated reform more than revolution which inevitably left a legacy of hatred, human suffering and destruction. In his early thirties, Butterfield was persuaded that the Christian interpreter, more than other political historians, was safeguarded against the worst illusions and idolatries, being prepared by his faith for accidents and surprises in history. By his worship of God, he was rescued from such distorting influences as a fanatical worship of the state, the idea of progress, or an abstract political ideology. By devotion to the ultimate ends of religion, the historian was enabled to understand

47

"...the web spun out of the play of time and circumstances...."[21] Providence held mankind under the judgment of God; yet God was not a tyrannical ruler but the source of grace in history. Even the clash of human wills reflecting man's pride and indestructible egotism could serve to further God's will and bring good out of evil. For example, the American Revolution led the British to invent a new and more civilized concept of empire. Man's most creative achievements were usually born out of human distress and inner pressures and political systems founded on brigandage, such as those of ancient Rome and the British Empire, might evolve in time in the direction of some tolerable measure of justice and order.

For Butterfield, therefore, historical studies and theology cohere and reinforce one another, for both have their center in a concern for human personalities. His dual emphasis on history and religion, however, has opened him to criticism from which he might have been spared had he followed the course of the traditional historian. Some critics see in his religious writings a diversion from the historian's primary task of producing a large corpus of solid historical writings such as might have resulted had he continued his research on Charles James Fox and George III. His position as scholar-statesman in the Cambridge University community, in which he lived and worked for more than a half century, culminating in his appointment as vice chancellor from 1959-1961, was certainly dependent to some degree upon his recognized preoccupation with moral values. His positions at Cambridge and his leadership roles in national and international educational bodies drew him away from full-time scholarship, as did the series of endowed lectures, characteristically on religious themes, in Germany, the United States, and the United Kingdom. Peter Geyl and other historians have questioned his emphasis on the persistence of evil in man's behavior and of human cupidity in society and his low estimate of the capacity of honorable men to effect social change through actions with certain and predictable consequences. This criticism of his questioning of the consequences of the moral and rational intentions of statesmen overlooks his debate with such twentieth century British historians such as Lewis Namier and his disciples, who portrayed politics largely as a struggle for gain and selfish interests. For Butterfield, ideas, attitudes, and rational intentions interact with self-interest in politics, and historians

err when they reduce politics for all individuals and
every century to the same dull level. The Namier
school, in so often assuming that politicians are no
more than the repository of self-interest, misinter-
prets political movements and political parties, which
do not merely advance group interests but also articulate values and ideals.

A more serious and partly legitimate criticism
of Butterfield's use of the Christian perspective has
been leveled at some of his historical judgments. In
Christianity and History, written after World War II,
he appeared to explain the defeat and destruction of
Germany as divine punishment for the sins of the German people. Yet critics ask: What of the many Germans who at grave personal risk opposed Hitler's
regime? And what about the Baltic peoples who had not
committed the brutalities of the Nazis, yet suffered
as grievously as the Germans? Butterfield has written
of the need for thinking historically at two different
levels, the level of technical history, which deals
with the limited and the mundane and takes into account
hard and tangible historical evidence, and the level of
Providence, which is beyond the reach of the technical
historian. Critics have maintained that Butterfield,
especially when he enters the realm of general history,
smuggles into his interpretations the Christian points
of emphasis and doctrine that he excludes from his
more technical writings in narrative history, where
he is more cautious in his assessments of individual
leaders. Worst of all, he sometimes appears to speak
for Providence whose divine words he merely notes and
records. In fairness, those critics who extract from
his writings moral valuations such as his indictment
of the entire German people contained in a wider
discussion of militarism will find him going on to say:
"...if Germany is under judgment so are all of us--the
whole of our existing order and the very fabric of our
civilisation."[22]

Finally, Butterfield's influence on Western thought
is not exhausted in his two major contributions to
traditional and Christian history. In 1958 he founded
the British Committee on the Theory of International
Politics and has served for approximately two decades
as its chairman and honorary chairman. This group took
as its mandate the making of an inquiry "...into the
nature of the international state-system, the assumptions and ideas of diplomacy, the principles of foreign
policy, the ethics of international relations and war."[23]

From the start the committee's approach reflected Butterfield's historical and religious orientation. The interests of this group of British thinkers contrasted with those of American colleagues who formed a similar committee, and its work expressed greater concern "...with the historical than the contemporary, with the normative than the scientific, with the philosophical than the methodological, with principles than with policy."[24] The themes of the group's first major publication mirrored Butterfield's own writings and included "Natural Law," "The New Diplomacy and Historical Diplomacy," "Society and Anarchy in International Relations," "Western Values in International Relations" and "The Balance of Power." Butterfield's closest associate in the venture, Martin Wight, introduced the volume with a paper entitled: "Why is there no International Theory?"

The British approach was the antithesis of that of flourishing schools in America and Australia that dealt with international relations theory and systems analysis. Its frame of reference was the conduct of diplomacy, international society, and the nation-state system. Its point of view was historical, empirical and deductive. Its underlying presuppositions assumed that historical continuities were more important than innovations in the international system; that statecraft provided an historical deposit of accumulated practical wisdom; that the classical writers in politics, diplomacy and law had not been superseded by recent findings in such disciplines as psychology and sociology; and that the corpus of earlier diplomatic and military experience was worthy of study and reformulation to meet contemporary needs. Undergirding the committee's work was a pervasive moral concern about which Butterfield wrote: "The underlying aim...is to clarify the principles of prudence and moral obligation which have held together the international society of states throughout its history, and still hold it together."[25]

The influence of Butterfield and the British committee has been greater in the United States than in Britain. American interst in the group's approach coincided with a mounting awareness in the 1950's and 1960's, first by a handful of political realists and later by decision-makers and journalists, that the struggle between the Soviet Union and the United States was too complex to define as a clash between absolute right and wrong. The conflict involved a profound

moral predicament, for even if the two super powers
were approximately equal in strength and virtue, each
could justifiably fear the other. Each could be sure
of its own good intentions without being able to trust
the other. Each could feel that its rival was with-
holding the one thing that could make it feel secure.
Each side in a conflict could pursue its security
through displays and threats of power, yet overlook the
fact that it could ensure its own security only by destroying the security of the other. For Butterfield
the security-power dilemma was the most urgent problem
of war and peace, and for him the only solution was
for one or the other great power to risk something
in the name of peace. The only way out of the worst
of deadlocks, he prophesied, was through some kind of
marginal experiment; but for such an experiment America would need the hard-level judgment of a hard-boiled
Bismark, not sentimentalists for whom giving way was
always too easy. Butterfield made his proposal more
than a decade before the Nixon-Kissinger policy of
detente was proclaimed. Butterfield approved this
policy and added that what was needed for accommodation
was a leader experienced in power politics and capable
of bold and subtle, yet hard-headed acts of political
and military judgment. He doubted that either a con-
ventional moralist or an ordinary intellectual or
idealist in the White House or in Whitehall could
succeed in formulating and defending a policy of
coexistence.

        In the United States the response to Butterfield's
ideas came from political realists. Although he can
be viewed as a spokesman for realism and practical
morality, Butterfield's realism has been tempered by
his profession as a historian and by Britian's ancient
tradition in foreign policy. Like Reinhold Niebuhr,
he has considerable influence on more thoughtful
leaders in the religious community, and has quoted the
Bible as often as he has historical texts applying its
wisdom to the realm of foreign policy. For Butterfield,
the enduring contribution of Christianity to the
requirements of international relations lies not so
much in the choosing of actual policies but in providing a background of ideas or a more civilized spirit
with which men can work. Christianity can help the
citizen to straighten out his ideas on human sin, to
recognize that although extraordinarily evil men do
exist, the most difficult problem in international
politics is the moderate cupidity of large numbers of
men who hope to realize through their nations what

society denies them as individuals. Such men exercise vast pressures on governments and make normalized relations among states more difficult. It is the main responsibility of religion to check the sovereign will of the people who want to achieve their objectives by too great an exercise of power, instead of by consciously cooperating with Providence.

In his appeal to American leaders in statecraft and religion to recognize their limits and to exercise prudence, Butterfield, writing at the height of the Cold War to a citizenry overanxious about the Soviet threat and imperiled by the risk of a thermonuclear holocaust, may have made his most lasting and valuable contribution.

[1] Sir Herbert Butterfield, The Historical Novel. (Cambridge, England: The University Press, 1924).

[2] Butterfield, The Peace Tactics of Napoleon, 1806-1808. (Cambridge, England: The University Press, 1929).

[3] Select Documents of European History, Vol. III, 1715-1920, ed. Butterfield. (New York: H. Holt & Co., 1931).

[4] Butterfield, George III, Lord North and the People. (London, England: G. Bell, 1949).

[5] Butterfield, George III and the Historians. (London, England: Collins, 1957).

[6] Butterfield, The Whig Interpretation of History. (London, England: G. Bell, 1931).

[7] Butterfield, Napoleon. (New York: Duckworth, 1939).

[8] Butterfield, The Englishman and His History. (Cambridge, England: The University Press, 1944).

[9] Butterfield, The Statecraft of Machiavelli. (London, England: G. Bell, 1940).

[10] Butterfield, Christianity and History. (London, England: G. Bell, 1949).

[11] Ibid., 5.

[12] Ibid., 6.

[13] Butterfield, Christianity in European History. (London, England: Oxford University Press, 1951).

[14] Butterfield, *History and Human Relations*. (London, England: Collins, 1951).

[15] Butterfield, *Christianity, Diplomacy and War*. (New York: Abingdon-Cokesbury Press, 1953).

[16] Buttefield, *The Origins of Modern Science*. (London, England: G. Bell, 1949).

[17] Butterfield, *Man on His Past*. (Cambridge, England: University Press, 1955).

[18] *The Historical Novel*, op. cit., 8.

[19] *Peace Tactics of Napoleon*, op. cit., vii.

[20] *The Whig Interpretation of History*, op. cit., 21.

[21] *Ibid.*, 66.

[22] *Christianity and History*, op. cit., 52.

[23] *Diplomatic Investigations: Essays in the Theory of International Relations*, ed. Butterfield and Martin Wight. (Cambridge, Massachusetts: Harvard University Press, 1966), 11.

[24] *Ibid.*, 12.

[25] *Ibid.*, 13.

ETHICS AND POWER IN INTERNATIONAL POLICY*

Michael Howard

Without doubt the most eminent of Sir Herbert
Butterfield's colleagues and disciples was Martin
Wight, his collaborator in organising the seminar spon-
sored by the Rockefeller Foundation out of which there
emerged the papers collected in the volume Diplomatic
Investigations (London 1966).

Wight, who died in 1972, was a remarkable man.
There has perhaps been no teacher in the field of international politics in our time whose approach to his
subject was more deeply serious or more erudite. There
have been many specialists more influential, more articulate and, regrettably, more prolific in their publications. Wight left behind him a lamentably small
number of writings, enough to give only a mere glimpse
of the qualities which so awed his pupils, his colleagues and his friends. He was a philosopher in the
oldest and best sense of the word: a man who sought
and loved wisdom. He was also a scholar in the oldest
and best sense: a man who loved learning. He was
above all a deeply committed Christian. He never for-
got--and I think quite literally never for a moment
forgot--that in the field of international politics one
is dealing with the very fundamentals of life and
death: with the beliefs, the habits, the structures
which shape moral communities and for which it is considered appropriate to die--and, worse, to kill. He
saw his subject neither as the interaction of abstract
state-entities nor as the equally abstract legal and
structural problems of international organisations,
but as the exercise of crushing responsibilities by
statesmen in an infinitely complex world; the conduct
of policies for which the ultimate sanction might have
to be war. And war was no matter of heroics or war-
gaming, but the deliberate infliction, and endurance,
of extremes of suffering as the ultimate test of the

---

*This article is based on the third Martin Wight Memo-
rial Lecture, given at Chatham House on January 12,
1977, and printed in International Affairs, (July
1977) vol. 53, p. 364.

validity of human institutions and beliefs. The work of some American 'behaviourists', who sought to reduce the vast and tragic tapestry of human affairs to elegant mathematical formulae was not simply repellent to him. It was unintelligible. He could not understand how people could do such things. He refused even to discuss it. For him, International Relations did not consist of a succession of problems to be solved in conformity with any overarching theory. Rather, like the whole of human life, it was a predicament: one to be intelligently analysed, where possible to be mitigated, but if necessary to be endured--and the more easily mitigated and endured if it could be understood. In his acceptance of the inescapably tragic nature of human destiny he was a thinker in a European tradition going back to that classical antiquity in which his own learning was so deeply rooted.

To superficial appearances Wight presented something of a contradiction. He accepted the fact, as he saw it, of 'Power Politics'. The brief study with this title which he wrote under the auspices of Chatham House in 1946, revised, enlarged and edited with an introduction by Hedley Bull and Carsten Holbraad, was republished in 1978. It is an almost defiantly traditional work, disdainful both of Liberal Utopianism and of the contributions of the behavioural scientists to the subject. It expounds the mechanisms of power politics in the international system without praise or condemnation: this is the way it has been, he implies, and there is no reason to suppose it could be otherwise. But at the same time he was a Christian pacifist and a conscientious objector, and no one who met him could be in any doubt of the profundity and the unshakeable firmness of the convictions on which his pacifism rested.

In actuality there was for him no contradiction. In a world of evil one must face the fact of evil and the need, in face of that fact, for the unfortunate Children of Darkness to be wise in their generation. In such a world statesmen and soldiers have responsibilities and duties which they cannot and should not seek to evade. Nevertheless in such a world it is the duty of some Christians to bear witness to a transcendent loyalty; and those on whom this duty is laid will know it in their inmost conscience and must fulfil it, irrespective of consequent embarrassment or hardship. Martin Wight's burning sincerity fused the apparent contradiction--not, probably, without much inner anguish--into a single coherent philosophy; one which

56

provided an analysis of the world predicament as much
as a guide to his own actions.

Wight was in fact a Christian pessimist, as were
so many of that generation which had seen the hopes of
the Locarno era wither, and who grew to maturity under
the shadow of the vast menaces of the 1930s. Even the
menaces of the 1950s, the perils, as they appeared at
the time, of nuclear holocaust, never loomed so large
in the eyes of contemporary observers. Those perils
could be, and indeed have been kept at bay by prudent
statesmanship. The nuclear danger is predictable and
controllable. But the 1930s saw the emergence of
forces of irrationality which it would be neither in-
appropriate nor hyperbolic to call forces of evil: unpredictable, uncontrollable, still only partially
understood. These forces fitted into the world picture neither of the Liberal humanists nor of the Marx-
ists. Both of these schools were children of eighteenth-century rationalism and nineteenth-century rad-
icalism. Each believed in its own way in inevitable
progress towards world democratic systems and had welcomed the overthrow of the militarist autocracies of
Central Europe as obstacles to the gradual conver-
gence of mankind towards unity and peace. But in
Fascism one was dealing with something consciously
beyond reason and defiant to reason--something of
which no secular ideology had hitherto taken account.

Christianity, unlike Liberalism or Marxism, did
provide an explanation; not the cheerful liberal humanitarian Christian teaching which read little into
the Bible except the Nativity and the Sermon on the
Mount, but the teaching which digested all the implications of the old Testament, including the prophetic
books, before turning to the New, which emphasised
that the Gospels themselves were full of uncompro-
misingly dark passages, and which faced the fact that
at the centre of the Christian religion, as of no
other great world religion, was a symbol of prolonged
and unavoidable suffering. The Christian eschatology,
long disdained by liberal humanists even within the
Church itself, once again became terrifyingly relevant
to human affairs. The works of Charles Williams, of
C. S. Lewis, and--drawing on yet wider sources of
Manichean myth--of J. R. Tolkien were deservedly popular as allegorical commentaries on the events of the
time. And the teachers who best provided an adequate
framework for understanding were the philosophers and
the theologians--Niebuhr, Bonhoeffer, Karl Barth,
Tillich--who accepted uncomplainingly the remoteness,

the inscrutability of God, who saw the focus of Christianity as the Passion rather than the Sermon on the Mount; men for whom the march of humanitarian, utilitarian liberalism, including its change of gear into Marxian socialism, had simply been a long excursion into the desert in pursuit of a mirage.

In the light of such a philosophy the accepted explanations of the problems of international politics and the causes of war all appeared inadequate to the point of superficiality. The received wisdom among liberal thinkers of the 1920s was that wars in general, and the First World War in particular, had been caused precisely by the operation of 'power politics' which in their turn reflected the prejudices of a militaristic ruling class and the interests of capitalist investors and armaments manufacturers. The solution lay in the abandonment of power politics conducted by means of secret diplomacy, and the adoption instead of programmes of collective security, arbitration, disarmament and the resolution of differences through open and reasoned discussion at the League of Nations. The problems which called for solution were those arising from the inequities of the Paris Peace Settlement, which was far too tainted with the evils of the old system. If only Germany could be reconciled and the injustices done to it undone, they believed then a new world order, a new era in the history of mankind, might be expected to dawn.

These ideas were reiterated in a deliberately simplistic form by publicists--E. D. Morel, Goldsworthy Lowes Dickinson, H. N. Brailsford, Leonard Woolf--who with some reason saw their first duty as the re-education of that public opinion on which they relied to make their dreams come true, but which had repeatedly shown itself prone to stubborn fits of xenophobia. Few of them were as naive as sometimes appears from their writings. The Royal Institute for International Affairs, Chatham House, was founded by a group which included not only such outstanding idealists as Lord Robert Cecil and Philip Noel-Baker but 'realists' of the stamp of Eyre Crowe and Neil Malcolm and such scholarly specialists as James Headlam-Morley and Arnold Toynbee; men who had discovered at Paris how terribly under-equipped the Allied statesmen were to deal with the tangled problems which victory had dumped in their laps, how vast was the distance which separated popular expectations from practical realities, and how important it was for the future peace of mankind that judgment on foreign affairs should be formulated on a basis of widely-shared expert knowledge.

Yet in broad terms these men certainly shared the aspirations of the liberal idealists. There was a broad ethical consensus that international politics should be conducted, not with the aim of maximising the national interest, but in order to enable mankind to live in a community of mutual tolerance and respect, settling its differences rationally, resolving its conflicts by peaceful means. This could best be achieved by the creation and management of international institutions, in particular the League of Nations; and by the education of public opinion in loyalties wider than narrow, old-fashioned patriotism. And finally Britain's own national affairs should be conducted in accordance with a Kantian categorical imperative, to provide an example for other nations and to smooth the path towards the development of a higher national community based on the rule of law. They would have accepted that it was their task to transcend the old order based on national power and to create a new one based on consent.

But what this generation did not fully appreciate was how far these values, the fine flower of Victorian Liberalism, was tied up with a social order and national institutions which might continue to need power, and in the last resort <u>military</u> power, for their survival. All had supported the Allied cause during the Great War on the not unwarranted assumption that its defeat would be a catastrophic setback to the progress of liberal ideas. All believed that responsibility for the war rested very largely with the militaristic ideology rooted in the quasi-feudal monarchical social order in Central Europe whose destruction had removed a serious obstacle to world peace. What was harder for them to appreciate was that the destruction of that order would not make easier the work of peace-loving bourgeoisie such as themselves, but infinitely more difficult: that it would create a vacuum to be filled by warring forces of revolution and counter-revolution out of which regimes would arise far more ferocious than those they had replaced--regimes even less susceptible to reason or enamoured of an order based on consent. It was the tragedy of the League of Nations, that consummation of a century of striving and dreaming, that it was founded at a moment when it could not hope to operate successfully except as the executive organ of a group of like-minded nations prepared in the last resort to enforce their decisions by precisely those mechanisms of military power which its very existence was intended to render obsolete.

59

The lesson was not lost on the men who had to reconstruct the international system after the Second
World War. They were more modest in their aspira-
tions--more modest also, it must be admitted, in their
talents. The new generation, at least in Britain, produced no one to equal the vigour and vision of the sur-
viving veterans, Toynbee, Webster, Lionel Curtis,
Philip Noel-Baker. The officials and the statesmen--
Strang, Jebb, Cadogan, Bevin--were the equals if not
the superiors of their predecessors; but there were no
seers to inspire them, no prophets of a new order. Only
one new academic figure of any eminence had been tempted
by wartime experience to reflect with any degree of profundity on the state of the world--Herbert Butterfield
himself; and he did so in terms which echoed the teaching of Reinhold Niebuhr across the Atlantic, and which
were to provide a continuing influence on Martin Wight.
There were certainly no British thinkers who believed
that the world was now theirs to mould; who felt, with
Dean Acheson, that they were "present at the Creation".
Perhaps the failure of the first creation was too fresh
in all their minds. But what was dominant in their
consciousness was the impotence, almost one might say
the irrelevance, of ethical aspirations in international
politics in the absence of that factor to which so little attention had been devoted by their more eminent
predecessors, to which indeed so many of them had been
instinctively hostile--military power: power not necessarily to impose their standards upon others (though
that, in the re-education of the defeated enemy, was
not irrelevant) but simply to ensure the survival of
the societies in which those ethical values were maintained. And to the vulnerability of such societies
and their value-systems a sad procession of emigré
scholars and statesmen from Central and Eastern Europe
bore eloquent witness--both before and after 1945.

This realisation of the impotence of ethical principle to operate unaided in a world of power does much
to explain the speed with which the world rearmed after
1950. The spirit of historical irony will record that
it was Mr. Attlee and his colleagues, not excepting
Sir Stafford Cripps, the very men who had voted and
spoken so eloquently in the 1930s against power politics and great national armaments, who now took the
decision to equip the United Kingdom as a nuclear power; that the Minister of Supply responsible for the
construction of the atomic bomb was Mr. John Wilmot--
the same John Wilmot whose election for the constituency

of East Fulham in 1934 had convinced Stanley Baldwin of
the impossibility of persuading the country to accept
a major rearmament programme; and that the Secretary of
State for Air in 1947, when the Air Ministry began to
design the bombers which would deliver the bombs, was
that most tireless and dedicated advocate of disarama-
ment, Mr. Philip Noel-Baker. And in the United States
liberals of equally impeccable antecedents, men who had
throughout their lives fought against American entan-
glement in the old world of power politics, now helped
to build up an armoury of terrifying strength in order
to 'defend the Free World'.

It is easy enough either to deplore this apparent
volte-face as a shameful betrayal of principle, or to
sneer at it as a belated acceptance of the facts of
life. But both reactions betray an attitude towards
political morality--indeed, towards social action as a
whole--which has although very widely held, proved
throughout history to be misleading. According to this
view, actions are to be judged against a single scale
which runs from the pole of 'power politics' at one end
to that of 'ethical action' at the other. Ethical considerations are held <u>automatically</u> to enfeeble power;
considerations of power are regarded as unavoidably
sullying ethics. It is an attitude no less popular
with professed 'men of the world' and 'realists' than
it is with idealists and reformers. The reluctance of
liberal critics seriously to examine the technical problems faced by the military--a reluctance as evident today as it was in the 1930s--is paralleled by the scep-
ticism with which a substantial number of officials,
soldiers and 'defence experts' regard the relevance of
ethical factors to the problems which they face. War,
they say, is war. Business is business. What needs to
be done, has to be done.[1]

The assumption that the exercise of coercive power
is in itself fundamentally immoral, and that involvement in power relationships automatically vitiates ethical behaviour, is natural enough. How can good ends
be served by evil means? How can one get peace by pre-
paring for war? How can all the mechanisms of military
power--the disciplining of soldiers, the development of
weapons, the training to kill, the posing of threats,
to say nothing of the awful actuality of warfare, shock-
ing enough in the pre-nuclear age, inconceivable today--
how can such activities conceivably contribute to ethical goals? Is not the whole 'power system' alien to
and irreconcilable with any ethical objectives except
those of the barbarian--and in adopting it even to fight

61

barbarians, is one not becoming a barbarian oneself?
To adopt the methods of coercive power--and economic
can be as debasing as military power--is in itself considered to be unethical, to debase the cause which
those methods are intended to serve.

Are ethics and power in fact such poles apart?
Most of us in practice do not consider that they are,
and within our own experience we can normally reconcile
them without too much difficulty. But this may simply
be the result of our own moral obtuseness and intellectual laziness. To provide a satisfactory conceptual
synthesis is not so easy. The long debate over raison
d'état, which Sir Herbert Butterfield took as the subject of the first Martin Wight Memorial Lecture[2] has
never been properly concluded. The tradition that led
through Plato and Machiavelli to Hegel, by which all
contradictions were resolved in service to a State
which was itself the highest value since it made possible all other values, disastrously popular as it became in Germany, has never been acceptable to Anglo-
Saxon Liberals--although the Marxist variant which for
'State' would substitute 'Revolution' succeeded in at-
tracting some of them in the 1930s. But perhaps a clue
to a more satisfactory formula can be found in the work
of another German thinker, albeit one who is seldom regarded as an authority on ethical questions: Karl von
Clausewitz.

Clausewitz did not indeed deal with ethical questions as such. He did not fundamentally question the
crude Machiavellianism of eighteenth-century politics:
the Grotian Law of Nations he dismissed as 'certain
self-imposed, imperceptible limitations hardly worth
mentioning, known as international law and custom'.
But on the relationship between war and politics he
did, as we know, have interesting and original things
to say; and these may provide useful guidance in any
consideration of the relationship between power and
ethics.

Clausewitz's theory was teleological. In warfare,
every engagement was planned to serve a tactical purpose. These tactical purposes were determined by the
requirements of strategy. The requirements of strategy
were determined by the object of the war; and the object of the war was determined by State policy, the
State being the highest embodiment of the values and
the interests of the community. Thus the objectives

of State policy ultimately dominated and determined
military means the whole way down the hierarchy of
strategy and tactics. War was not an independent
entity with a value-system of its own.

For Clausewitz State policy was the ultimate mover
and justification, the criterion by which all other
actions were to be judged--which in itself would make
his doctrine as it stands unacceptable to the liberal.
But what if one introduces one further, and ultimate,
step in the hierarchy, to which State policy itself
should be subordinated--the ethical goal? The State
itself then becomes not an end but the means to an
end. It has a dual role. It exists primarily to enable its own citizens to realise their ethical values;
but it exists also to make possible an international
community of mankind, whose values and interests are
ultimately determinant, not only of State policy as
such, but of all the means, military and otherwise,
that are used to implement State policy.

Such a pattern goes beyond that 'Grotian' concept
of international relations of which Hedley Bull spoke
in the second Martin Wight Lecture;[3] for although in
the Grotian formulation States are governed by a 'Law
of Nations' which is based partly on a reflection of
the divine order and partly on prudential considerations of self-preservation, they need no justification for their policy beyond the requirements of their
own existence. They accept a law of nations as man
accepts the laws of a just society: because his own
needs dictate that he should do so. But in the Clau-
sewitzian formulation, as we have elaborated it, State
policy would be determined by and judged according to
the needs of the international community. In the
same way as war, if it were not directed by State policy, would be 'a senseless thing without an object',
so State interests and State policy would make no sense
and have no justification if they were not shaped in
accordance with the overriding needs of mankind. As
military power is subordinated to and guided by State
policy, so State power should be subordinated to the
political object, true: but the military had its own
requirements. It had to work according to its own
inner necessities. Only the military specialist could
determine whether the goals set by policy were attainable, and if so what the requirements were for attaining them. Military affairs had, as Clausewitz put it,
their own grammar, even if they were subordinated to
political logic; and the grammar was intricate and

ineluctable. Armed forces require bases, and those
bases may only be available in countries with which
one would, for ethical reasons, prefer not to be allied.
National industry, on which military capacity is based,
may require access to raw materials available only
from countries which are equally politically embarrass-
ing. The successful conduct of the most just and de-
fensive of wars may demand alliance with States whose
price is the support of war aims which flatly contra-
dict all one's own normative values--as did for example those of Italy in the Treaty of London in 1915,
that last and most notorious example of power politics
and secret diplomacy. Yet rather than yield to Italian demands on Slav territory, would it have been
morally preferable for the Entente Powers to have
waived the Italian alliance, leaving the Central Powers
with their hand free to deal with Russia, and thus pro-
longing the war if not risking outright defeat?

One can multiply examples endlessly; let me concentrate simply on one. In 1935 there occurred a su-
perb opportunity for Britain to shape its policy in
the service of an ethical objective: the implementation of its obligations under the Covenant of the
League of Nations by imposing penal sanctions upon
Italy in order to deter or punish its aggression
against Abyssinia. Not only was the crime unambiguous:
the criminal was highly vulnerable. Public opinion,
in the 'Peace Ballot', had recently expressed itself
in favour of mandatory sanctions, even at the risk of
war. The case might have been deliberately created to
test the effectiveness of that new system of collective
security and the rule of law which had been brought
into being since 1918 to replace the old chaotic system of power politics. It would have been a perfect
example of the use of coercive means to attain political ends.

We can now see that there were many reasons why
the British government flinched from the test; but
certainly not the least was the uncompromising and
unanimous opposition of those experts in military
grammar, the Chiefs of Staff. Within the power structure which it was their duty to operate there were
two far more serious threats, not simply to the rule
of law in international politics, but to the security
of Britain and its Empire: the growing power of Nazi
Germany and the increasingly open aggression of Japan.
To risk even successful war against Italy would have
been to enfeeble the already pathetically weak fleet

64

available to deter Japanese attack in the Far East,
and to antagonise a potential ally whose help was, in
the eyes of France if not of Britain, indispensable
in containing the German threat. The military grammar
appeared unanswerable; it was to be that, rather than
the ethical imperatives of collective security, which
determined State policy.

In retrospect one can say that even in their own
terms the military grammarians may have got it wrong.
Faced with the real prospect of war Mussolini might
very easily have retreated; his catastrophic humilia-
tion would probably have imposed a high degree of cau-
tion both on Germany and Japan; a pattern of peace-
keeping would have been successfully established. But
the arguments of the grammarians could not simply be
overriden. The ethical imperative could not be, in
Clausewitz's words, 'a despotic lawgiver'. In the last
resort the statesmen were, as ever, faced with a balance of imponderables, with problems to which there
were no clear-cut ethical solutions.

To say, therefore, that State policy should be
subordinated to the ethical imperative as strategic
considerations should be subordinated to State policy
does not get us very far. The world of power remains
stubbornly autonomous; the suzerainty of ethics may be
of quite Merovingian ineffectiveness. Moreover such a
formulation can lend itself to the crudest of casuis-
tical justification of all coercive means in terms of
the ethical end--of police torture of political dissidents in order to preserve a stable and orderly society,
of the Soviet invasion of Czechoslovakia in 1968 in
order to preserve the stability of Eastern Europe, of
the 'destabilisation' of Chile to maintain the stability of the Western hemisphere, of the secret bombing of
Cambodia to maintain the independence of South Vietnam.
Because such actions may be dictated by the grammar of
coercive power, they cannot--any more than can terror-
istic destruction of life and property or intimidatory
guerrilla massacres--be justified, i.e. made in themselves ethical, by an ethical object. The dimensions
of power and ethics remain stubbornly different.

Indeed, so long as we think of power and ethics
in terms of dimensions, we may not go too far wrong.
Dimensions do not contradtict one another, nor can
they be subordinated to one another. They are mutually
complementary. Political acitivity takes place in a
two-dimensional field--a field which can be defined by

the two co-ordinates of ethics and power. The ethical co-ordinate (which we may appropriately conceive as vertical) indicates the purposes which should govern political action: the achievement of a harmonious society of mankind in which conflicts can be peacefully resolved and a community of cultures peacefully co-exist within which every individual can find fulfillment. The horizontal co-ordinate measures the capacity of each actor to impose its will on the environment, whether by economic, military or psychological pressures. Movement along this co-ordinate, the increase or decrease in coercive capability, has as such no dimension of morality, any more than does any elevation of moral standards necessarily involve an increase in one's power to implement them. One may become more powerful without becoming in any way less good.

Effective political action needs to take constant account of both dimensions. To concern oneself with ethical values to the total exclusion of any practical activity in the dimension of power is to abdicate responsibility for shaping the course of affairs. To accumulate coercive power without concern for its ethical ends is the course of the gangster, of St. Augustine's robber bands. Indeed it could be argued that each of these unidimensional courses is self-defeating; that the co-ordinates, if indefinitely prolonged, become circular. Obsession with ethical values with no concern for their implementation is ultimately unethical in its lack of practical concern for the course taken by society; concern for coercive capability without the legitimisation of moral acceptance leads ultimately to impotence, and disaster at the hands of an indignant and alienated world. Thus political action, whether in the international or any other sphere of activity, needs to be diagonal. Ethical goals should become more ambitious as political capability increases. The political actor, be he statesman or soldier, needs to grow in moral awareness and responsibility as he grows in power. The moralist must accept that his teaching will not reach beyond the page on which it is written or the lectern from which it is expounded without a massive amount of complex activity by men of affairs operating on the plane of their own expertise. The more ambitious and wide-ranging the ethical goals, the greater the power-mechanisms required to achieve them.

In pursuing his diagonal course the statesman is like a pilot reading a compass bearing from which he must not diverge in either direction if he is to achieve his goal. Too rigorous a concern for moral absolutes may reduce or destroy his capacity for effective action. Yet to ignore such norms entirely may gain him short-term advantages at the cost of ultimately reducing his capacity to operate effectively in a world made up, not of robber bands, but of States functioning as moral as well as military entities, whose authority is as dependent on moral acceptability as on coercive capability. He may have to commit or authorise acts which, as a private citizen, he would deeply deplore. No one involved, for example, in the repatriation of Soviet troops from British-occupied Europe to Russia immediately after the Second World War could have felt anything other than distress bordering on misery at the need for such action. But in the political dimension the object of maintaining friendly relations with the Soviet Union in order to achieve yet wider ethical objectives--the peaceful settlement of Europe and of the world as a whole--had to be regarded as mandatory. To call attention to the ethical problems created by such actions is appropriate and necessary; but they cannot be condemned on such grounds unless account is taken of the political dimension as well.

Acton was being less than fair to the world of politics when he declared that power tends to corrupt. What does tend to happen, as I suggested earlier, is that the grammar of power, so intricate, so compelling, becomes for those who operate it a universe in itself-- as indeed for the moralist and the reformer, the ethical objective can become an exclusive obsession which makes him disdain the tedious and murky problem of how to attain it. Yet perhaps there is a kind of gravitational force, against which statesmen have consciously to fight, which keeps their activities always closer to the horizontal co-ordinate of power than to the vertical one of ethics, which constantly weighs down their efforts to maintain the diagonal. Overloaded political decision-makers and members of huge bureaucracies have enough to contend with in day-to-day management of affairs without constantly searching their consciences as to the ethical implications of their actions. That makes it all the more important that their ethical perceptions should be internalised and operate automatically and continuously. Government departments seldom carry a chaplain on their establishment to provide an ethical input into policy-making.

The appropriate response of the political moralist to the world of power must therefore be not to condemn but to enlighten, to understand, and to acknowledge and accept that the Children of Darkness have a painfully-learned wisdom in their own generation which is deserving of respect. As Niebuhr put it, 'Politics will, to the end of history, be an area where con-science and power meet, where the ethical and coercive factors of human life will interpenetrate and work out their tenative and uneasy compromises.'4 As a thinker whose ideas were deeply rooted in ethical values, Martin Wight knew that even he could make no serious contribu-tion to the study of international politics without first attaining a full understanding of the coercive factors operating within it. But he never ceased to look beyond these 'uneasy compromises' to the ultimate goal of full and final reconciliation.

And if the editor of this volume may speak for himself and Professor Howard: "Neither has Sir Herbert ever stopped his quest for the relationship of prac-tical necessity and ultimate meaning."

FOOTNOTES

[1]Although in my experience defence specialists are
more likely to be concerned about questions of ethics
than are 'peace researchers' and liberal reformers
about the problems, either fundamental or techical,
of military or any other kind of power. It is significant that association by universities with the
Ministry of Defence in Britain, or with the Pentagon
or the Central Intelligence Agency in the United States,
is regarded by many students as being immoral almost
by definition, and one is regarded as extremely naive
if one ventures to ask why.

[2]Given at the University of Sussex on April 23,
1975.

[3]Reprinted in the British Journal of International
Studies, Vol. 2, no. 2, (July 1976), 101-116.

[4]Reinhold Niebhur, Moral Man and Immoral Society:
A Study in Ethics and Politics. (New York: Charles
Scribner's Sons, 1949; first published in 1932), 4.

TOLERATION IN RELIGION AND POLITICS

Adam Watson

Herbert Butterfield has dealt both with history
and international politics and their interrelationship
with international morality. At the center of Butterfield's concern is the question of the role of religion
in international affairs. Within this general context
he has occupied himself over the years particularly with
the Reformation and its effects on the European states
system.

This is not the whole range of the impact of religion on international relations: it is a particular
example. There are two main aspects of his interest in
this example, which dovetail into one another. Firstly,
there is his lifelong interest in religious conflict:
how and why it began, and especially how and why it
ended. Those who are familiar with his major books,
such as Christianity and History, Christianity, Diplomacy and War, and particularly The Whig Interpretation
of History, will remember how basically concerned they
are with this issue, and how regularly the struggles
which followed the Reformation are used to illustrate
his themes. Secondly, there is Butterfield's equally
sustained interest in statecraft. He has contributed as
much as any scholar now living to óur understanding of
the real nature of the relations of states to one another, princes and republics alike; and notably the extent of their awareness, or disregard, of being members
of the Republica Christiana, the Public Interest of
Christendom--what later came to be called Europe. So
we have his books on the Statecraft of Machiavelli, on
Napoleon; his interest in Richelieu; and his studies of
Raison d'Etat and the Balance of Power.

So with these two interests, religious conflict and
statecraft, playing on one another, it was inevitable
that his thought, again and again, should come back to
toleration. And one can see how, looking at the problems
of today, since the Second World War, his interest is
caught by the ideological conflict on the one hand and
the statecraft on the other, and drawn to the question
of toleration between the two ideologies, Western and
Soviet, that opposed each other in the Cold War.

At this point some people will legitimately wonder whether it isn't very dangerous simply to transpose what happened in the Wars of Religion to the present ideological struggle. Are not the two contexts too different for that? Indeed, Butterfield is much too serious a historian to take models from the past out of their context and use them as a ready-made analysis of the current situation, let alone as guides to conduct in our present predicament, in the way that Machiavelli for instance did with incidents from Greek and Roman history. Indeed the whole of The Whig Interpretation of History, and much of Butterfield's other writing, combats the idea that history is the struggle of the goodies against the baddies, the story of progress winning out against reaction, or of one side being more for liberty, as we understand it, than the other. Butterfield insists that our liberties come from the clash, and from the ruin caused by the clash, which drove men to look at the whole issue in a different light.

This brings us to Toleration. Here I mean toleration of evil in spite of your sincere belief that it is evil.

"Toleration" said Butterfield in a paper on Toleration in Early Modern Times[1] "can perhaps best be reguarded as a system or a régime. It was not so much an ideal, a positive end, that people wanted to establish for its own sake; but, rather, a pis aller, a retreat to the next best thing, a last resort for those who often still hated one another, but found it impossible to go on fighting any more. It was hardly even an "idea" for the most part--just a happening--the sort of thing that happens when no choice is left and there is no hope of further struggle being worthwhile. During the second half of the sixteenth century there were both Catholics and Protestants who became Politiques, declaring that persecution was the ideal but that the bloodshed must be ended. The body politic itself was being destroyed, and further conflict would make the tragedy irremediable." The politique attitude was denounced by the hardliners on both sides. "Up to the beginning of the eighteenth century, the word tolérance had, in French, a pejorative meaning: it signified a lax complacency towards evil. In 1691, in his admonition to the Protestants (VIe Avertissement aux protestants III, ix), Bossuet still proudly described Catholicism as the least tolerant of all religions; and as if to compete with his proud boast, the Walloon Synod of Leyden (an overwhelming majority of whose members were Huguenot refugees)

72

firmly condemned religious toleration as a heresy. The Huguenot preachers of mid-sixteenth century France were determined not to condemn religious persecution as such, even though it was they themselves who were bound to be the sufferers from it for the time being."

The Politiques were, then, people for whom other things, the things of this world, mattered more than right and wrong. Butterfield has always been interested in them, and in the part they played in the drift towards toleration. In The Whig Interpretation, written in 1931, he says: "Parties like the politiques in France acknowledged that one religion alone could be the true one, but said the state must not be wrecked for the sake of religion. In these cases Toleration comes as a secular ideal. It is the reassertion of the rights of society and the rights of this world, against beliefs which by their warfare and by the absoluteness of their claims were acting in defiance of social consequences. Elizabeth of England, Catherine de Medici (Butterfield likes to remark how often these politiques were women) William the Silent, Wallenstein attempted to heal the sorrows of the time and to overcome the Reformation tragedy by subordinating religion to policy. They helped the cause of liberty because they were too worldly, and from the point of view of their own age they were too wicked, to support one set of beliefs or another in defiance of social consequences, and in disregard of a public good."

However, Butterfield is even more interested in the people who still passionately believe, who see the other side as the real danger--the real contamination of mankind--and still stop fighting--people who came to long for peace and détente for fear of the consequences of continuing the struggle. "At the back of everything, moving men to this revision of ideals, was the tragedy of the Reformation, the havoc caused by the existence of two forms of religion in the same society. The question that exercises the next generation will be how at least to contrive that religious controversy shall not spread ruin over the world."

So toleration comes, not through any belief in freedom of religion, and certainly not from thinking that religion doesn't matter, not even from a positive belief in peace. It comes in spite of a nagging sense among weary believers that they were failing in their duty, that they were craven, or worldly wise. Their consciences were pulled by preachers like John Bunyan who exhorted them to continue the good fight and to be valiant against all disaster. But they could not go on.

Religious toleration came in the end through exhaustion: spiritual as well as material. And this exhaustion made room for raison d'état. I will come back to raison d'état in a moment. I want now to look at what Butterfield has to say about the idea--the age old assumption--that a community should have only one ideology, should be dedicated to only one set of propositions; and that it is precisely this which makes a society one. The following quotations are taken from both Toleration in Early Modern Times and the Waley Cohen Memorial Lecture on the Historical Development of the Principle of Toleration in British Life. The relevance of his comments to the contemporary scene is obvious. Indeed so striking is this relevance that I want to repeat Butterfield's injunction not to make too facile a comparison with this or that incident in the past, but rather to see the whole process as throwing light on our predicament today.

"It is necessary to carry our eyes back to the time when religion was the bond of the tribe, and the solidarity of the nation was exhibited in the corporate relationship which it established with its deity. A new stage of development would appear to be reached when a people which has begun by thinking that its god is above all other gods proceeds to the discovery that He is, in fact, the only God who really exists. Such a people can now become more conscious that, in its relationship with God, it is finding contact with the Absolute; and religion develops a new kind of exclusiveness, claiming to be unique but asserting also its universal validity."

"In the ancient world it seems to have been in the nature of religion that it should be an affair of the whole community, but this might not necessarily prevent a people from adopting further gods from neighbours, allies and conquered territory, nor did it prevent what the literature of the Babylonians, the Hittites and the Old Testament suggest to have been touching personal relationships between individuals and some particular deity. Amongst the ancient Jews there appears, especially after the passage into Exile--appears very specifically in the prophecies of Ezekiel, for example--a

74

stronger emphasis on the private wire between the individual and God; while in the period before Christ,
various sects like the Pharisees, the Sadducees and the
Essenes seem to have emerged without breaking the unity
of the essential faith; and there were some Jews who
believed and some who disbelieved, in Resurrection.
All this was calculated to produce fructifying tensions
in religious life. But the coming of Christianity re-
vealed the limits of what Judaism could accept, and
opened a period of greater tolerance."

In this less tolerant age, following the establishment of Christianity, it was not through the call of
belief on individuals that communities were converted
to new religions, dedicated to new propositions and new
creeds.

"We have to face the fact that, after the fall of
the Roman Empire, a barbarian Europe was Christianized
to a considerable degree by a process of mass-conversion,
by military conquest or governmental command. Amongst
such barbarian peoples this may have been the best thing
that could have happened, and the only thing that any
religion could have achieved; but the process was not
entirely unlike the one by which another great section
of the globe was to become Mohammedan or that by which
a great part of Europe and Asian have been brought over
to Communism in our time. In some respects, it im-
plied a reversion to the spirit and methods of pagan
systems, and it was bound to be accompanied--though
not necessarily at all points--by a corrupting of the
religion itself. Furthermore, by the force of custom,
the monopoly of education, the combined pressures of
society, the imposing character of authority, and the
alliance of governments, such a system, once established, could endure for centuries. It is possible
that during most of these centuries hardly anybody
would feel that he was being regimented or oppressed."

So, when we come to the Reformation and the
division of Christendom, we can understand why, if the
states, "the monarchies of Europe, were to recognise
the coexistence on the Continent of two forms of
religion, it was likely to be very difficult to go on
maintaining any notion of a Christendom. But if, within each separate monarchy rival forms of belief were
allowed to coexist, it would be very difficult indeed
to maintain the ideal of the State."

"It was not the leaders of the Reformation, who brought--or intended to bring--religious liberty (in the sense that we understand it) to Western Europe. Here we must be careful not to impute to men of former ages the purposes and the intellectual assumptions which are natural to us at the present day. The great reformers were moved not by the passion for individual freedom but by a burning anxiety to see right religion established in the world. In the sixteenth century, when God was not a mere hypothesis and hell not a speculative affair, the question of the right religion tended to be not only the most momentous but also the most immediately urgent thing in life. Even if we believe that behind the actions of men there is always a vested interest, we must realize that here was an interest at least as powerful in its effect on human motive and human conduct as the mundane things which are the object of cupidity at the present day. And nobody can begin to understand the overfacing difficulty of the problem of religious toleration who fails to enter into the psychology of this situation, and to realize that the problem concerns men who believe in religion as an absolute thing--all of them being unanimous in the view that only one religion can be right. In all ages the problem of religious liberty (which would otherwise be an easy one) requires to be treated with due respect for this fundamental fact.

"The leaders of the Reformation did not capture Christendom; they only half-succeeded, and the cause of liberty owes as much to their failure as to their success. A tremendous problem, an impossible paradox, resulted from the deadlock that was produced. The Continent was confronted with two forms of Christianity--two exclusive religions--each claiming to embody the absolute truth, each asserting itself to be essential to salvation, each regarding the other as a diabolical perversion and a menace to human society. When we today see the Communist half of the world ranged against what we call the Liberal half, we are sometimes tempted to imagine that here is the absolute logical impasse--the rival doctrines can never meet, the parties can never compromise, the systems are mutually exclusive, neither of them can rest, neither of them can feel safe, until the other is annihilated. Let us be clear that it is just this absolute impasse which has existed in the past--has existed with double intensity and double the difficulty because the confrontation was between parties both of which were obsessed by religion. It led to some of the most

bitter warfare in modern history, and in the interludes
between these struggles there were all the phenomena of
the endless, unrelenting 'cold war.' Ideological conflict even produced some of the development and patterns that have become familiar in our time--such things
as Fifth-columnism and Collaborationism. It required
a creative act to produce a way round this impasse--
there had to be changes in many things besides Catholicism and Protestantism, changes perhaps in one's view
of the role of religion in society, changes in one's
notion of the place of the individual in the world. But
there could be no change in the fundamental fact that
a truly religious man who walks with God and lays hold
on the spiritual life believes that he has found contact
with the eternal verities--believes, therefore, that his
religion is true in an absolute sense. If this had not
been fundamental to the situation, there would not have
been a problem to solve."

"Paradoxically enough, the atrocities that occurred
in the wars of religion and the civil dissensions must
be attributed to ideas which practically all the warring
parties held in common.

"Wherever it was established, it became clear that
toleration, as a working system, was subject to serious
limitations. Its own upholders tended to regard it as
only a temporary expedient--a thing necessary perhaps
until a General Council of the Church had met and
established a new order. Alternatively, there was an
assumption that after a period of generous treatment,
the heretics would voluntarily return to the fold.
Even in France, where perhaps the history of toleration
proved the most remarkable, there remained a persistent
Catholic view that the heretics would sooner or later
come back to the Church of Rome. Even Richelieu, who
had taken from the Huguenots the military and political
privileges which had turned them into "a State within
the State"--privileges which were making the work of
government very difficult--seriously felt that by leaving them with their religious privileges intact, even
though they had been defeated in war, he had shown a
generosity which would win them over in the long run to
the true religion.

"A neater way of disposing of the divisions in
religious belief was the policy of "comprehension"
which, while envisaging a broader kind of Church that

would embrace both parties, involved some negotiation
for a kind of compromise. This way of recovering unity
was the one most congenial to the heads of great monarchies.

"In France, an extraordinarily difficult situation
arose, partly because various groups of reformers (some
of them not clearly heretics) secured patronage at first
in high places, while the King, not always the friend of
the Pope, was able to hope that the dissenting bodies
could be a support to his diplomacy. When at last, in
1559, the King found it necessary to turn his attention
seriously to the religious problem, it turned out that
he had neglected the matter too long, and he could not
cope with the size of the movement, or with the insurrec-
tionary character that it had been developing. In the
last four decades of the sixteenth century the Catholics
and Huguenots represented parties both of which on a
number of occasions were stronger than the Crown--the
monarch being able to save himself only by making
alliance now with one and now with the other. In France
there developed in fact what might properly be called
"the Ulster situation"; and no man should pretend to
have policies for such a predicament, unless he has
studied the last four decades of French history in the
sixteenth century, including the massacre of St. Bar-
tholomew.

"The Huguenots became powerful enough to exact from
the government, not only toleration, by royal edict and
in practice, but also the right to have armies and
troops to defend their possession of it. Here, more
than anywhere else, a system of toleration had to be
accepted because the country and the government realised
that further war would mean, not victory for anybody but
just the defeat of France."

"The first religious settlement in Germany, in 1555
after civil war, confined its benefits to Catholics and
Lutherans, but established the principle of cuius regio
eius religio. It did not allow religious variations
within single states, but under what seems to us today
a civilized arrangement, permitted the dissidents of
either party to move to a principality which had established the form of religion they preferred." But the
practice of toleration soon developed inside principal-
ities in Germany. Fifteen years later the Emperor
Maximilian tolerated first Lutherans and then all dis-
senters in Austria. Perhaps he thought that even

heretic subjects were preferable, in wordly terms, to a wholesale emigration of talent. As the generations succeeded one another, it became less acceptable to persecute people who simply adhered to the faith of their parents, whatever this might be.

"Long before the sixteenth century, the Church had been ready to grant an exceptional toleration to Jews, and to those who had been brought up in paganism. This practice is recognised by St. Thomas Aquinas and was brought into currency by humanists who wanted a more liberal treatment of offenders. A similar liberty was naturally desired on occasion by heretics themselves, who claiming to be Christian believers of a sort, did not see why they should not be treated as generously as Jews and unbelievers. As the decades passed, there were Catholics in the Reformation struggles who felt that Protestants of the second or third generation could hardly be persecuted for adhering to the faith in which they had been brought up."

In spite of this grudging toleration, Butterfield field sums up the cold war period of the religious struggle in Europe on a somber note--a passage that reminds us forcibly of our own cold war.

"The Reformation itself did not lead to religious liberty. It issued rather in the principle cujus regio ejus religio, so that in the nation or the smaller regional units, the prince or the noble or the effective government decided which of the competing systems was to prevail. There was toleration for governments in a sense, one might say; but only because none of the contending parties could capture the Continent and bring the nations back to uniformity--only because there existed no higher authority capable of preventing governments in general from doing what they liked. Each political unit tended to become a separate religious society therefore, but insisting still on a corporate worship, on solidarity in the faith, on religion as the bond of the tribe. It was this that made it so difficult to contemplate the policy of toleration inside any of the politico-religious units. The most liberal thing you could do, when policy was based on such a footing, was to make your single national Church as wide and comprehensive as possible; but even in England this attempt was proving unsuccessful--it left unreconciled parties on both wings--in the reign of Queen Elizabeth herself. In reality, the régime of cujus regio ejus religio would seem to have produced greater

bondage for the individual--that is, the dissident
individual--than had existed at all widely before the
Reformation. The authority of a distant papacy was
superseded--or, alternatively, was reinforced--by the
severer control of the local government. The oppres-
sion was greater because the tyrant was more close at
hand."

In due course, then, the exhaustion, the weariness
with the struggle, the sense of ever increasing desola-
tion and ruin, produced two attitudes of mind which
helped to overcome the religious conflict. One was
raison d'état. The other was not exactly religious
indifference, perhaps not even a real abatement of
religious animosity; simply a feeling that other considerations also counted, and legitimately counted.

Raison d'état was for statesmen, for rulers.
Ragione di stato, what might be called the arguments of
state, began in Italy as a rather mundane and even
shameful regard for temporal advantage. But it gradually became, especially in the minds of people like
Queen Elizabeth and Cardinal Richelieu, a sense of
responsibility towards the state which God had called
them to rule or administer, a feeling that the welfare
of the people, and indeed the material wealth, under
their charge required decisions of a special kind.
These decisions had to be calculated rationally. And
this reason, what was right for the state (the word
raison means both reason and right) was an obligation
on the ruler, a categorical imperative so to speak,
which ought to override his personal convictions and
inclinations. So Henri IV, lifelong champion of the
Huguenots as he was, decided that "Paris vaut bien une
messe", so that he could, as he said, put a chicken
back into the cooking pot of every peasant in France.
So Richelieu, devout as he was, felt it necessary to
ally France with all the Protestant powers of Europe,
not to mention the Infidel Turk, against the Catholic
Habsburgs. And so in the name of raison d'état the
Calvinist Dutch agreed not to oppose the Cardinal's
military suppression of the Huguenot state-within-a-
state, because they needed a strong France to save the
Netherlands from Habsburg hegemony. This right and
reason of state was a subtle thing. It was to be distinguished from the obligations of a man as a private
individual, on the one hand, and from the doctrines of
religion on the other. It came to be argued that a
ruler might and should do things for the public weal
that he must not do for his own advantage. Of course

this doctrine--the ancestor of the National Interest--
is subject to perversion and abuse. But it enabled the
Secular State, as Butterfield says, "to rise above the
religious parties and compel them to make peace. Mundane considerations made toleration appear as the only
policy." It is obvious what part the modern equivalent
of raison d'état has played and still plays in producing the détente in Europe, in abating the cold war.

The other attitude of mind was more elusive, more
difficult to define in the post-Reformation period, and
more elusive in Europe today. It is wrong to call it
ideological indifference. That was the attitude, some
would say the sin, of the politiques who were tired of
religious wrangling. And there are politiques in the
ideological quarrels of today. But there are others,
as there were in the seventeenth century, who are
sincere believers, who still on Sundays, so to speak,
adhere to the true faith, and sincerely mean to struggle
harder against what the hymn calls the troops of Midian
who prowl around; but somehow, during the week, are
more faint hearted and shrewder headed. So today there
are many who, whatever their ideological commitment,
are swayed by the new wind that is blowing in Europe, in
favor of ideological tolerance. Here Butterfield likes
to quote W. K. Jordan's book, The Development of Toleration in England. "Professor Jordan," he says, "makes
a remark particularly relevant to the study of religion,
and especially the examination of the transition taking
place in the sixteenth and seventeenth centuries. It
should be regarded as an important corrective of the
straight lines of causation which so often over-simplify
the passage from one period to another. He writes:

> The historian of ideas, at least,
> must ever realise that a dozen works
> written in the heat of controversy,
> or a score of pamphlets indited by
> secretaries gripped by a blinding
> fear, may not, despite their blind-
> ing intensity, be so significant as
> indices of the nature of cultural
> change as the cold verdict of a judge
> on assize, the casual quip of a Pepys,
> or the blunt observation of the squire
> to his lady.[2]

In the kind of case that Professor Jordan has in mind,
the historical transition to which we are tempted to

attach a too simple linear cause, ought rather to be
seen as a gradual change of texture taking place in a
complicated piece of material."

Butterfield goes on to say that "the German
physicist and Nobel prize-winner Heisenberg, who once
spent a good deal of time in Cambridge, discussed with
me on various occasions a point that he loved to make:
namely that the scientific revolution of the sixteenth
and seventeenth centuries--these very centuries of the
wars of religion--was really due to a general change,
but a subtle change, in man's feeling for matter--this
matter not being a quasi-mystical, quasi-magical thing
any longer, but sluggish and inert, lying motionless
unless a person happened to do something to it. In
other words, Heisenberg attributed a peculiar causative
importance not to the passage of an idea from one
writer to another, but to something that can be described as a more general change of texture.... In
the early part of the sixteenth century it was regarded
as entirely natural that the stars, the planets and the
heavenly bodies in general, were composed of a special
ethereal kind of matter, not like anything on the cum-
brous and rugged earth--not subject indeed to weight or
friction or chemical analysis. But within a century or
so it was just as natural for everybody to feel that
the stuff the planets were made of was essentially the
same as our earthy kind of matter, and the obvious
result of this was that the scope of science itself was
mightily enlarged. Yet I am not clear that it was any
book or any demonstration that directly generated this
particular change of feeling about matter. I would
judge that a score of separate things had made people
come to feel differently about the heavens. There
had occurred a different way of experiencing things.

"This aspect of the changes that take place with
the passage of time is not less remarkable in the sphere
of general religious beliefs."

I hope that the passages I have quoted from
Herbert Butterfield's writings on religious toleration,
and what I have said as well, will have made the implications for our own ideological conflict generally
pretty clear. In any case Butterfield would be hor-
rified at too close an analogy, too simple a parallel.
He would only want to indicate the motive forces, the
absence of victory for either side, the mundanity, the

weariness, by which the equivalent of toleration can come about, perhaps is coming about, today. Let me list four propositions of this kind, which may help to indicate this process, this development in the contemporary scene.

First, we can see now, as we saw in the Reformation and Wars of Religion, ideological conflict and statecraft, contrary forces but dovetailed into each other, opposed but interlocked. We can see the politiques raising up mundane considerations, economic advantage in particular--the Mercutios who cry "a plague on both your houses" about the Montagues and the Capulets in whose quarrels they are destroyed.

Secondly, we can see today men who sincerely believe in one creed, one ideology or the other, yet fear that the ideological struggle may get out of hand. There are the "next generation" who in Butterfield's phrase "want to contrive that ideological controversy shall not spread ruin over the world." Today it is the awesome prospect of nuclear war in particular that these honest men fear, and legitimately fear, as they see that it might destroy the whole northern hemisphere. Though they deeply believe the other side to be evil, yet they see no policy goal, no national interest, only the transcendental conflict of good against evil itself, which could justify such a cataclysm as a nuclear conflict between the two superpowers. The historian Clausewitz distilled from his experience of Napoleon's wars the conclusion that to resort to war is to continue the pursuit of policy goals with the addition of other means. But what policy goal can be served by the certain annihilation of oneself and one's own state?

Thirdly, the continent of Europe has again been divided, much as the Holy Roman Empire was in 1555, into states whose governments maintain one ideology or the other, and whose peoples have to conform or at least find themselves excluded from office and authority if they dissent, perhaps more than before 1914. Cuius regio eius religio is again a fashionable formula. And as then we now have individuals on both sides of the line who dissent, who want a change; whose sympathies-- open or secret--are not perhaps with the other side as a political power, but with the other ideology in a general sense, yes.

Finally, in Europe--all Europe, from the Atlantic to the Soviet border--we can see how increasingly weary

men and women are of the ideological struggle. There
is a subtle shift in the texture, the climate of ideas.
This is not just a question of détente, of relaxation
of ideological tensions. Europeans sense, perhaps half
aware, that the whole argument matters less than it did.

Let me take two countries that are in some ways
(but certainly not all) the mirror image of each other:
Italy and Poland. In the one we have the government
of the state in the hands of the Catholic party, the
Christian Democrats; but so strong is the hold of the
other great party, the Communists, that it is impracticable to govern Italy without at least a tacit "compro-
messo storico", an understanding, a toleration, perhaps
even a discreet collaboration in certain fields. In
Poland the government of the state is, as a consequence
of the Second World War, in the hands of the Communists;
but so powerful is the Catholic church there that it is
impracticable to govern Poland either without that minimum of informal tolerance and even more tacit coopera-
tion which is required to make the governance of the
state possible. So the texture of men's minds shifts,
even if they cling to their ideological convictions.

Raison d'état, impelling statesmen to make alli-
ances across the ideological divide, helps this process:
but it is a revaluation that occurs in its own right.
And in turn this climate of opinion supplements the
hunch of statesmen that the real issue is not communism and capitalism any more: that the conflict between
the Soviet world and the West has more to do with power
politics. And for those of us in Europe who are not
citizens of either superpower, the essential problem in
external relations within our war-scarred continent is
no longer how to change the formal status quo, but how
to live with it. Can we make life and thought more
comfortable, and contacts across the lines easier, can
we tolerate what we disapprove of, tolerate it rather
shamefacedly perhaps, in order to lessen the burden of
ideology and the weight of the superpowers on us?

Of course if you put the question in specific
terms to most people, they will tell you of their belief
in freedom and democracy or in scientific socialism.
And they will mean it. Especially, so to speak, they
will mean it on Sundays, and in public statements. But
it is already observable that they no longer act accord-
ingly. Their minds and aspirations are already moving
along new channels.

This is toleration without condoning what you
believe is wicked and dangerous, toleration through
spiritual exhaustion. It is not a very noble thing,
admittedly. But out of it something more worthwhile
may grow.

FOOTNOTES

[1]A paper delivered at a conference organized by
the Giorgio Cini Foundation in Venice, in conjunction
with The Journal of the History of Ideas.

[2]W.K. Jordan, The Development of Toleration in
England, II ie 1640-1660 (194).

III

Ethics and Contemporary Problems

MORALISM AND AMERICAN FOREIGN RELATIONS

Norman A. Graebner

That characteristic which has distinguished American foreign policy from that of every other major power in the twentieth century is its repeated assertion of moral purpose. This approach to policy stems from the belief in a moral political order, derived from universally valid principles of freedom and justice. It places blame for the faults of civilization not on the basic nature or man and politics, but on the perversity and wickedness of certain isolated groups or nations. Americans who have favored the application of this faith to foreign policy have believed that the United States could achieve a more perfect international society through the power of its idealistic purpose. They have attributed to American idealism a specific force in world affairs capable of altering the behavior of other nations. Under the lash of American moral strictures other governments presumably would admit their morally inferior position and thereafter pursue policies that conformed to American will. Woodrow Wilson expected no less of American policy. "It is a very perilous thing," he told a Mobile audience in October, 1913, "to determine the foreign policy of a nation in the terms of material interest. It not only is unfair to those with whom you are dealing, but it is degrading as regards your own action.... We dare not turn from the principle that morality and not expediency is the thing that must guide us, and that we will never condone iniquity because it is most convenient to do so." Arguing for such standards in American foreign relations. Thomas Cook and Malcolm Moos, asserted in their book, Power Through Purpose (1954): "We must bid for world leadership on the ground that we represent a moral order and purpose which, by reason of its own binding logic, imposes no dogma and demands no conformity beyond commitment to the method of freedom." To acknowledge the permanency of power politics, they insisted, would fail "to make American foreign policy a continuation, a projection, and a fulfillment of those ethical purposes which Americans have long professed and pursued."

Behind this utopian strain in American foreign policy was both a sense of democratic mission and an

89

illusion of omnipotence that flowed from the country's
easy successes of the nineteenth century. In response
to such conditioning, American leadership often concerned itself only with ends. Following the Spanish
American War, it assumed commitments which, for the
first time in American history, exceeded the nation's
power. In the acquisition of the Philippines and in
the Open Door policy for China, the United States
welcomed obligations which it had no intention of sup-
porting with actual power. Already the country was
exposing itself to attack in the western Pacific, for
empire demands its price. Undaunted by its expanding
commitments, all rationalized by concerns for humanity,
the United States quickly universalized its moral intentions. From the tradition of rationalism embodied
in democratic practice came also the goals of peace
and self-determination for all peoples. Under Wilson
the United States became at last the agency for
achieving the peaceful promise of the twentieth century--
a world free of power politics, the balance of power,
and heavy military expenditures. For American leaders
the question of means for achieving such purposes was no
longer a subject of debate or discussion. Moral purpose would generate its own strength, for it was in
league with the innate desires of all peoples.

Unfortunately foreign policies anchored to democratic principles (principles always more easily ver-
balized than achieved even where law theoretically
prevailed) rather than to power and the minimum demands
of national interest ignored both the diplomatic history
of the modern world and those precepts of external relations which had guided the successful policies of the
nations of Europe and the United States. The first
principle assumed that imperfections in world politics
derived from the weaknesses of human nature, from the
persistence of force, and from the perennial clash of
national interests. It insisted that each country
recognized the competition of others and attempt to
guide them through force and diplomacy toward a more
stable and peaceful society. It recognized no challenge as the final evil that remained in the path to
utopia, realizing that universal peace and justice had
never characterized world society and probably never
would. Second, since no country was omnipotent, the
essential method of foreign policy was that of hoarding
resources and power by pursuing goals limited to the
nation's interests. Its purpose was to keep small wars
small so that the limited power and resources of a
nation would not be overtaxed. War might change the

distribution of power but it would never eliminate its
use. Thus the nation's objectives abroad were always
best determined by the immediate and long-term costs
of their achievement.

Walter Lippmann had written that

> a foreign policy consists in bringing
> into balance, with a comfortable surplus
> of power in reserve, the nation's com-
> mitments and the nation's power. The
> constant preoccupation of the true
> statesman is to achieve and maintain this
> balance. Having determined the for-
> eign commitments which are vitally
> necessary to his people, he will never
> rest until he has mustered the force
> to cover them. In assaying ideals,
> interests and ambitions which are to
> be asserted abroad, his measure of their
> validity will be the force he can mus-
> ter at home combined with the support
> he can find abroad among other nations
> which have similar ideals, interests,
> and ambitions.

Since commitments abroad must always be limited by
available power, no obligation, political or commercial,
could be maintained unless the nation was willing to
pay the price. As Thucydides wrote, "You cannot
decline the burdens of empire and still expect to share
its honours." Thus was essential that a government
take stock of its assets and liabilities so that it
would not promise its own people more than it could
achieve, not demand of its allies more than they might
willingly contribute, or of its opponents more than
the balance of power might force them to concede.

Power and its proper use has underwritten the
success of all political systems. Thomas Jefferson
anticipated the future growth of the United States but
wondered whether it would always use its power effectively. He wrote: "Not in our day, but at no distant
day, we may shake a rod over the heads of all, which may
make the stoutest tremble. But I hope our wisdom will
grow with our power, and teach us that the less we use
power, the greater it will be." Since all countries
have interests and commitments for which they will go
to war, power and the techniques of diplomacy should
be kept in proper balance in the pursuit of rational and

achievable goals. The relationship of force to compromise is well illustrated in a Moon Mullins cartoon. The
elderly representative of the utopian school asks Kayo:
"Remember the golden rule. Now, supposing that boy
slapped you on the right cheek, what would you do?"
Kayo replies realistically, "Jest how big a boy are you
supposin?" It was reality of power and conflicting
purpose in determining the course of world affairs that
traditionally forced statesmen to seek temporary and
imperfect settlements of conflicts, not their total
removal, because they knew that the elimination of one
problem would merely open the gates for others.

It is not strange that moralistic behavior in
international life has a near-perfect record of failure.
Whereas all successful statesmen of the modern world
pursued their nations' interests through the methods of
power and diplomacy, the great moralists in world
affairs have never achieved their goals. Why they in-
variably failed to protect the interests of their
countries or conserve the expenditure of force is clear
enough. Refusing to concern themselves with the concrete issues raised by pressures for change, they
adopted objectives that soared beyond their national
interests and became, in like measure, unachievable
through diplomatic means. Whatever their claims to
moral superiority, policy goals based on abstract
principles of self-determination and peaceful change
demand capitulation of all who would defy the established treaty structure with force. By insisting that
change, to be legitimate, must be limited by general
agreement, they enshrined the status quo and thereby
granted the right to determine the course of history,
not to the stronger, but to those who possessed. Thus
the moralistic approach to international relations
denies the role of force in the creation and main-
tenance of the existing order. Specific circumstances
determine whether any elaborate moral defense of the
status quo conforms to the national interest of those
countries who uphold it, but the determination to prevent all unwanted change through moral strictures
eliminates diplomacy as an acceptable means for resolving major international controversies. Under the imperative of moral principles which place all jsutice on the
side of established treaty arrangements, a national
leadership, in effect, foreswears foreign policy itself.
For if a foreign policy consists of a program designed
to achieve some obtainable goal, then a foreign policy
based on moral objectives which are not attainable is
not a foreign policy at all. It is a collection of

92

phrases, perhaps popular, but nonetheless irrelevant. For example, Franklin D. Roosevelt's demands on both Germany and Japan after 1937, anchored to moral defenses of the status quo, simply eliminated American diplomacy from the search for peace.

Experience teaches that wars fought to achieve some moral purpose are easily transformed into crusades, because moralism places an antagonist in an immoral and uncivilized position. Only the moralist can threaten civilization in the name of morality; the realist is less sure of his monopoly of the right, less sure that utopia will spring from the ashes of war. The realist is tolerant of evil because he knows that he cannot uproot it. Crusading for some moral objective not only makes war inevitable but also makes it limitless. William Graham Sumner, the American sociologist, once observed:

> If you want war, nourish a doctrine.
> Doctrines are the most frightful ty-
> rants to which men ever are subject,
> because doctrines get inside of a
> man's own reason and betray him against
> himself. Civilized men have done their
> fiercest fighting for doctrines....
> A doctrine is an abstract principle; it
> is necessarily absolute in its scope and
> an absolute, and the affairs of men are
> all conditional and relative.... What
> can be more contrary to sound states-
> manship and common sense than to put
> forth an abstract assertion which has
> no definite relation to any interest of
> ours now at stake, but which has in it
> any number of possibilities of produc-
> ing complications which we cannot foresee,
> but which are sure to be embarrassing
> when they arise!

Similarly, Winston Churchill cautioned those who would claim special virtue in their desire to punish those judged to be depraved: "The human race cannot make progress without idealism, but idealism at other people's expense and without regard to the consequences of ruin and slaughter which fall upon millions of humble homes cannot be considered as its highest or noblest form."

World War I became so destructive of civilization because leaders ignored Europ's cultural unity and

93

the limits of human society. Having gone to war from convictions of innocence, the democracies could not forgive the enemy. By making the initial act of hostility the pretext for drastic policy, they ceased to think of objectives and consequences. In their moralism they transferred all the evil of international society to the enemy of the moment. Thus the war was fought not to limit hysteria and the employment of force, but to give them maximum scope. As a crusade for righteousness the war could admit of no compromise; it could not end short of unconditional surrender. Precisely because it defied the great traditions of the past, that war succeeded in destroying or weakening the security of all who sought to achieve the new utopia of peace and freedom. Instead of eliminating war, the struggle gave to war a dreadful character which it had never before attained. And, as Herbert Butterfield wrote in the aftermath, "since we cannot yet say that we have produced a world in which the possibility of war is at all ruled out, it is a question whether a more terrible moral responsibility does not lie upon those who insisted on war a outrance than on those who had perhaps only the marginal responsibility for the outbreak of hostilities in the first place." Specifically that war laid the foundations for a new nationalism in Germany, it provoked the Russian revolution, it sapped the strength of Britain and France, it destroyed the possibilities of political stability in Eastern Europe, it deepened national resentments and helped to usher in a new age of barbarism. The rise of fascism and Communism as threats to Western democratic tradition, the Second World War itself, the rise of Russia to greater continental predominance than Germany ever enjoyed, and the constant threat of global war all arise out of conditions produced by the war which begain in 1914.

At the height of its power the United States was more beset with danger and fear than ever before in its history. Yet its power to influence the world environment remained decidedly limited. Communism may die, but if it does it will not be because the United States so willed it, but because humankind in general willed it. And if the world ever becomes genuinely democratic, it will occur because democracy, more than any other political system, coincides with the basic desires of human beings. Through tolerance and goodwill the United States might yet seek to create a relaxed world in which the normal drives of human beings will have that opportunity of finding their way upward toward freedom and democracy. When progress does occur, leaders dare not boast that changes beneficial to a people were the result of American moral indignation, or pour scorn and ridicule on those who seem to be losing their grip on their populations. George F. Kennan pleaded in Harper's of August, 1956, when the ties of the Soviet bloc appeared to be loosening:

> Let us not, in particular, discourage evolution in this new direction by receiving it with wild boasts that it represents the triumph and vindication of our policies and an ignominious defeat for the Soviet leaders who have introduced these changes. The victories of democracy occur not when men are destroyed, but when they are illuminated and made wiser and more tolerant. If greater liberality now comes to the Soviet world, the victory belongs not to us but to the forces of health and hope that live--thank God--in men everywhere, however they may at times be thrust down and discouraged; and if a defeat has been suffered, it was not really by the men who brought about these changes, but by those tendencies within their own system--perhaps within their own minds--that were unworthy of any great people and unresponsive to men's deepest needs. Let us have the humility to recognize these things, let us remember we are the agents, not the authors, of the eternal verities in which we profess to believe, and let us not take personal credit for what is in reality the power of these verities themselves.

What sustained the illusions of American power and influence in world affairs through the present century was the failure of leadership to recognize the unique sources of power that gave the United States its earlier successes. American spokesmen forgot that after 1900 the United States no longer played on a continental stage where it always had the strategic advantage. No longer in the new century did it find the barriers to the triumph of its will in Indians, plains, mountains, Spain, or Mexico. England was the only major threat to American security before 1900, and the United States was wise enough to settle its differences with that

95

nation through diplomacy and accommodation. In this century the Republic faced such new accretions of power as Germany, Russia, China, and Japan, and it faced them on issues that lay in the Eastern and not the Western Hemisphere. At no time after 1900 were America's unique nineteenth-century sources of power operative. Any marked achievements in America's diplomatic history have rested on force and diplomatic maneuver, not on the willingness of other nations to respond to charges of illegality and immorality. It would be difficult to find any precise achievement of American idealism when embodied in foreign policy; it is exceedingly difficult to touch even the slightest problems in areas not under direct political control. Whenever the American fiat has been effective abroad it was because American purpose rested on clearly demonstrable interests and the power to achieve.

Yet as late as the 1960s the United States demanded the liberation of mainland China and the Russian satellites. When the nation failed to achieve such goals, Americans in large numbers refused to admit their hopelessness in the real world of diplomacy and criticized the nation's leadership for not being firm enough. One well-known American businessman chided the Kennedy administration for not conducting its foreign policy with the moral determination of Theodore Roosevelt. If Roosevelt could free the American Greek, Ion Perdicaris, by threatening the Sultan of Morocco, why should the United States settle for less than total surrender from the Kremlin? One author suggested that the United States government take a lesson from the TV Western heroes. Would a Wild Bill Hickok, a Lone Ranger, or a Matt Dillon take from their law-breaking opponents what the United States tolerated in the behavior of Russia and China? With characteristic American utopianism the script writer always assures the viewers of TV westerns that justice will win and at no cost. Countless numbers of American citizens viewed foreign policy through decades as if some script writer would similarly guarantee the triumph of American purpose everywhere around the globe.

Moral abstractions have repeatedly rendered American foreign policy threatening or meaningless. Yet their popularity continues in both high places and low. The reasons are many. Moralism, the assumption that the nation can have its way with words alone, makes it easy for a leadership to be complacent, to avoid the role of instruction, to ignore the complexities of international

96

life, to escape the need for precise knowledge of other
countries and the problems and ambitions that motivate
them. Moralistic declarations of purpose, in short,
become a technique, especially effective in democracies,
for simplifying all issues and avoiding all responsibility for what occurs. They satisfy those who demand success with a minimum of cost and risk. It is easier to
close the gap between commitments and power--for it must
be closed at least for the sake of appearances--with
moralistic strictures than with actual power. Moralism
is the perfect approach to foreign policy for an isola-
tionist nation, for it allows the government to avoid
specific obligations which might infringe on freedom of
choice. Moralism, finally, fits the political folklore
of the American people who for decades have been assured
that they have a special mission to fulfill of carrying
freedom and justice to the four corners of the earth.

To establish the ends of policy, even in utopian
terms, is neither difficult nor costly. It requires no
great effort to declare, especially from some political
platform, that the United States demands a world in which
all countries, but especially the antagonists of the
moment, will adopt policies that conform to American
principles. Yet once such objectives have been regis-
tered through public pronouncement or through political
debate, there is no escape. The government is under
the obligation to move toward their realization. It
is subjected to the psychological and political pressures that always come to bear upon leaders when a
particular achievement is expected of them. Government
must make progress toward its declared goals or bear
the charges of failure. Even if the goals are meaningless in the world of reality, officials must still keep
alive the illusion that triumph is at hand. In this
demand for success, whatever the goal, lies the American
dilemma. Citizens of the United States might view their
personal affairs with stark realism, but in foreign
affairs they have been taught to expect perfect perfor-
mance at little cost. If they understood the nature of
the world in which they live, they would not emerge from
every major period of crisis disillusioned and determined
to escape the world. They would not expect utopia beyond every diplomatic and military bout, but rather
would be prepared for new power arrangements and new
challenges which always follow major power struggles.
The world would cease to be an everlasting puzzle. And
if they recognize the maximum role of power and the
minimum role of idealism in world affairs, they would
be realistic enough to withstand the propaganda of those
at home and abroad who play upon their disillusionment.

Realistic foreign policy finds its answer in accommodation. It discovers its morality in the attempt
to achieve what is possible through diplomacy, realizing
that it is better to achieve partial good than to court
calamity in the pursuit of principle. Moralistic purpose not backed by power or the inclination to compromise the issues at stake will achieve nothing or it will
achieve war. In the process of attempting to achieve
what it cannot achieve, it destroys the very moral
values that it sets out to promote. Because it is derived from a false antithesis between morality and
power politics, it arrogates to itself all moral values
and places the stigma of immorality upon the theory and
practice of power politics. It would appear that genuine
morality, if it favors the lessening of tension and the
avoidance of war, must rest on the side of those who would
would avoid moralizing and devote their intelligence and
power to the achievement of what their limited national
interests will permit. A policy that achieves some good
through diplomacy is more defensible than one that persistently disappoints the expectations of those who have
taken the appealing but overdemanding rhetoric seriously.

HUMAN RIGHTS & FOREIGN POLICY[*]

Hans J. Morgenthau

A professor of law at Harvard at the beginning of
the century said that, with the exception perhaps of
theology, there is nothing about which so much non-
sense has been written as international law. One could
add to this statement or one could modify this statement by extending it to international morality. There
has been recently a flood of statements, some of them
on the highest authority, that have very little to do
with a philosophic or even pragmatic understanding of
international morality. Let me say first of all, in
criticism of those who deny that moral principles are
applicable to international politics, that all human
actions in some way are subject to moral judgment. We
cannot act but morally because we are men. Animals
are limited by their own nature; they don't need and
they don't have moral limitations that restrain their
actions. But man, exactly because his imagination
soars above natural limits and his aspirations aim at
certain objectives that are not naturally limited,
must submit as man to moral limitations that may be
larger or more narrow as the case may be, but which
exist.

Take an example from the conduct of foreign policy
and you will see right away that this cannot be otherwise. At the Conference of Teheran in 1943, in the
presence of Roosevelt and Churchill, Stalin suggested
that the German general staff be liquidated. I quote
Churchill's report:

> The whole force of Hitler's mighty
> armies depended upon about 50,000
> officers and technicians. If these
> were rounded up and shot at the end
> of the war, German military strength
> would be extirpated. On this I thought

---

[*] This paper was originally delivered as the First
Distinguished CRIA Lecture on Morality and Foreign
Policy and published by the Council on Religion and
International Affairs in 1979.

it right to say the British Parliament and public will never tolerate
mass executions even if in war, in
war passion, they allow them to begin.
They would turn violently against
those responsible after the first
butchery had taken place. The Soviets
must be under no delusion on this
point. Stalin, however, perhaps
only in mischief, pursued the subject.
"Fifty thousand," he said "must be
shot." I was deeply injured. "I
would rather," I said, "be taken out
into the garden here and now and be
shot myself than sully my own and my
country's honor by such infamy."

Obviously, here you have as clear an example as one
can wish of a moral reaction to a particular course suggested in foreign policy. Whenever we are face to face
with a situation in which a statesman could perform a
certain action that would be in his interest and he
refrains from doing so, he acts under a moral compul-
sion. Take any number of examples from history and
you will see that time and again statesmen have refrained from certain actions on moral grounds, actions
they could have taken physically and which would have
been in their interests.

Take, for instance, the sanctity of human life in
peace, which we today take for granted. This is a
development that is relatively new and didn't exist, for
instance, in the fifteenth or sixteenth centuries. At
that time it was common to kill foreign statesmen who
were particularly obnoxious to oneself. The republic
of Venice had a special official, the so-called official poisoner of the republic of Venice--we have the
records, everything was written down, because obviously
they were not afraid of congressional investigations--
and we can read that one poisoner was hired on proba-
tion and was assigned Emperor Maximillian and tried five
times to kill him without success. The record does not
show whether he was hired or let go.

In any event, at that time the killing of foreign
statesmen or foreign diplomats was as common a practice
among nations as is today, let me say, the exchange of
notes or summit meetings. Until very recently we have
refrained from such practices. We have witnessed in

this particular and in other respects a moral improve-
ment in the behavior of nations--which, it is obvious,
is in the process of disappearing. That is to say, we
are living in a situation in which the moral restraints
that in the eighteenth and nineteenth centuries contributed greatly to the civilized relations among nations
are in the process of weakening, if not disappearing.

Let me give you another example, an obvious one.
Take the distinction that has been made in the
eighteenth and nineteenth and the beginning of the
twentieth century between combatants on the one hand
and noncombatants on the other. The Hague and the
Geneva conventions laid down intricate legal rules of
conduct, which in turn are a reflection of moral rules
of conduct to the effect that only soldiers ready to
fight shall be the object of belligerent action but
that soldiers who want to surrender, or who are inca-
pacitated, and civilians altogether shall be exampt
from warfare.

In the First World War it was still regarded as
outrageous that certain armies would deal harshly with
certain groups of the civilian population. Still, at
the beginning of the Second World War an outcry of
indignation swept through the Western world when the
Germans bombarded Coventry, Rotterdam, Warsaw. At
the end of the Second World War we accepted the destruction of the major German cities and of Hiroshima and
Nagasaki with considerable equanimity. Here again what
you see is a decline in the adherence to moral values in
general. But in any event it cannot be doubted that the
conduct of foreign policy is not an enterprise devoid
of moral significance. That is, like all human activities, it partakes of the judgment made by other actors
and witnesses to the act when they perceive the act.
To say this is perhaps to belabor the obvious.

To conclude from this omnipresence of the moral
element in foreign policy that a country has a mission
to apply its own moral principles to the rest of humanity or to certain segments of humanity is quite something else. For there exists an enormous gap between
the judgment we apply to ourselves, our own actions, and
the universal application of our own standards of action
to others. Take again so elemental and obvious a principle of action--obvious at least and elemental for
us--as the respect for human life and the refusal to
take human life except under the most extraordinary,

exculpating circumstances. There are obviously civilizations and even groups within our own civilization
that have a much less strict conception of the sanctity
of human life, that are much more generous in spending
the life of others than we would be and would have been
under similar circumstances.

So there exists of necessity a relativism in the
relation between moral principles and foreign policy that
one cannot overlook if one wants to do justice to the
principles of morality in international politics. The
relativism is twofold. It is a relativism in time (to
which I have already referred), when certain principles
are applicable in one period of history and not applicable in another period of history, and it is a relativism in terms of culture--of contemporaneous culture--in
that certain principles are obeyed by certain nations,
by certain political civilizations, and are not obeyed
by others.

That consideration brings me to the popular issue
with which the problem of morality in foreign policy
presents us today, and that is the issue of what is now
called human rights. That is to say, to what extent is
a nation entitled and obligated to impose its moral
principles upon other nations? To what extent is it
both morally just and intellectually tenable to apply
principles we hold dear to other nations that, for a
number of reasons, are impervious to them? It is
obvious that the attempt to impose so-called human
rights upon others or to punish others for not observ-
ing human rights assumes that human rights are of universal validity--that, in other words, all nations or
all peoples living in different nations would embrace
human rights if they knew they existed and that in any
event they are as inalienable in their character as the
Declaration of Independence declares them to be.

I'm not here entering into a discussion of the
theological or strictly philosophic nature of human
rights. I only want to make the point that whatever
one's conception of that theological or philosophical
nature, those human rights are filtered through the
intermediary of historic and social circumstances, which
will lead to different results in different times and
under different circumstances. One need only look at
the unique character of the American polity and at these
very special nowhere-else-to-be-found characteristics
of our protection of human rights within the confines
of America. You have only to look at the complete

102

lack of respect for human rights in many nations, or in
most nations (consider that there is only one black
country in Africa with a plural political system; all
others are dictatorships of different kinds) to realize
how daring--or how ignorant if you will, which can also
be daring--an attempt it is to impose upon the rest of
the world the respect for human rights or in particular
to punish other nations for not showing respect for
human rights. What we are seeing here is an abstract
principle we happen to hold dear, which we happen to
have put to a considerable extent into practice,
presented to the rest of mankind not for imitation but
for acceptance.

It is quite wrong to assume that his has been the
American tradition. It has not been the American tradition at all. Quite the contrary. I think it was
John Quincy Adams who made the point forcefully that
it was not for the United States to impose its own principles of government upon the rest of mankind, but,
rather, to attract the rest of mankind through the example of the United States. And this has indeed been
the persisting principle the United States has followed.
We have made a point from the very beginning in saying
that the American Revolution, to quote Thomas Paine,
"was not made for America alone, but for mankind," but
that those universal principles the United States had
put into practice were not to be exported by fire and
sword if necessary, but they were to be presented to
the rest of the world through the successful example of
the United States. This has been the great difference
between the early conception of America and its relations to the rest of the world on the one hand and what
you might call the Wilsonian conception on the other.

For Wilson wanted to make the world safe for democracy. He wanted to transform the world through the will
of the United States. The Founding Fathers wanted to
present to the nations of the world an example of what
man can do and called upon them to do it. So there is
here a fundamental difference, both philosophic and
political, between the present agitation in favor of
human rights as a universal principle to be brought
by the United States to the rest of the world and the
dedication to human rights as an example to be offered
to other nations--which is, I think, a better example
of the American tradition than the Wilsonian one.

There are two other objections that must be made
against the Wilsonian conception. One is the

impossibility of enforcing the universal application of
human rights. We can tell the Soviet Union, and we
should from time to time tell the Soviet Union, that its
treatment of minorities is incompatible with our conception of human rights. But once we have said this we
will find that there is very little we can do to put
this statement into practice. For history has shown
that the Soviet Union may yield under certain conditions
to private pressure (and I have myself had certain experiences in this field; the agitation in which I was
involved, for instance, in favor of the dancers Panov
had a great deal to do, I think, with the final release
of that couple). There are other examples where private
pressure--for example, the shaming of public high officials in the Soviet Union by private pressure--has had
an obvious result. But it is inconceivable I would say
on general grounds, and more particularly in view of the
experiences we have had, to expect that the Soviet Union
will yield to public pressures when public pressures
becomes an instrument of foreign policy and will thereby
admit its own weakness in this particular field and the
priority of the other side as well. So there is, I
think, a considerable confusion in our theory and
practice of human rights, especially vis-à-vis other
nations in the field of foreign policy.

There is a second weakness of this approach, which
is that the United States is a great power with manifold
interests throughout the world, of which human rights is
only one and not the most important one, and the United
States is incapable of consistently following the path
of defense of human rights without maneuvering itself
into a Quixotic position. This is obvious already in
our discriminating treatment of, let me say, South
Korea on the one hand and the Soviet Union on the other.
Or you could mention mainland China on the one hand and
the Soviet Union on the other. We dare to criticize and
affront the Soviet Union because our relations, in spite
of being called detente, are not particularly friendly.
We have a great interest in continuing the normalization
of our relations with mainland China, and for this
reason we are not going to hurt her feelings. On the
other hand South Korea is an ally of the United States;
it is attributed a considerable military importance,
and so we are not going to do anything to harm those
relations.

In other words, the principle of the defense of
human rights cannot be consistently applied in foreign
policy because it can and it must come in conflict with

104

other interests that may be more important than the defense of human rights in a particular instance. And to say--as the undersecretary of state said the other day--that the defense of human rights must be woven into the fabric of American foreign policy is, of course, an attempt to conceal the actual impossibility of consistently pursuing the defense of human rights. And once you fail to defend human rights in a particular instance, you have given up the defense of human rights and you have accepted another principle to guide your actions. And this is indeed what has happened and is bound to happen if you are not a Don Quixote who foolishly but consistently follows a disastrous path of action.

So you see that there are two basic logical and pragmatic hindrances to a consistent policy of the defense of human rights. On the one hand you cannot be consistent in the defense of human rights, since it is not your prime business as a state among other states to defend human rights, and second you cannot pursue human rights without taking into consideration other aspects of your relations with other nations, which may be more important than those connected with human rights.

Where does it leave us in the end? I think in this consideration of the relations of foreign policy and morality we are in the presence not of a peculiar, extraordinary situation but of a particular manifestation of a general human condition. As I said at the beginning, we are all moral beings because we are men. And we all try to a greater or lesser extent--to a better or worse extent one might say--to realize the moral principles with which we are identified. We find that we are faced with contradictions, with difficulties--logical, pragmatic, moral difficulties themselves. And so the best we can do is what Abraham Lincoln asked us to do. He warned us first against the exaggeration of moral virtue we claim for ourselves, and next he outlined the limits within which man can act morally and at the same time have a chance for success. Lincoln's statement was made during the Civil War and is a reply to a petition by a delegation of ministers who asked him to emancipate all slaves forthwith: Here is what Lincoln said:

> In great contests each party claims
> to act in accordance with the will
> of God. Both may be and one must

be wrong. God cannot be for and
against the same thing at the same
time. I'm approached with the most
opposite opinions and advice and that
by religious men who are equally certain that they represent the divine
will. I'm sure that either the one
or the other class is mistaken in that
belief and perhaps in some respects,
both. I hope it will not be irreverent
for me to say that if it is probable
that God would reveal his will to
others on a point so connected with my
duty it might be supposed he would
reveal it directly to me. For unless
I am more deceived in myself than I
often am it is my earnest desire to
know the will of Providence in this
matter and if I can learn what it will
be I will do it. These are not, however,
the days of miracles and I suppose it
will be granted that I am not to expect
a direct revelation. I must study
the plain physical facts of the case,
ascertain what is possible and learn
what appears to be wise and right.

THE TRANSCENDENT AND THE RELATIVE
IN MORALITY AND FOREIGN POLICY*

Kenneth W. Thompson

Every discussion of ethics and politics or ethics
and foreign policy comes down in the end to a debate
over a transcendent as against a relativist ethics.
This issue is raised so repeatedly because for every
purpose served by an ethical system, different claims
can be and are made. Does such a system provide principles which can serve as guides to action? What are
the standards it seeks to establish? How viable and
relevant to the social order is the set of principles
it brings forward? What kind of ordering of priorities
among ethical and political principles takes place
within the ethical system? How does such ordering
relate to mankind's most urgent problems? What are the
inner consistencies of a given ethical theory and its
essential coherence as a body of thought? And if we
accept the proposition of the Harvard philosopher,
John Rawls, that a "theory however elegant or economical must be rejected or revised if it is untrue," what
can we say about the truth of a given ethical theory?

1. Guides to Action

In both law and political philosophy the natural
law tradition has been praised as affording answers to
these questions. As the stars and the planets in the
heavens are guided by natural laws that hold them in
orbit and assure their harmonious movement, man's right
relationships in the social and political universe are
said to be guided by natural law. As science has pen-
etrated the mysteries of the physical universe and
broken through the veil of ignorance, so human reason
will be able to discover and explain the natural laws
of the social universe for the guidance of men. Justice requires that human relationships be conducted in
accordance with the precepts of nature independent of

_____

*This paper is an abbreviated version of a chapter in
a forthcoming book by the author, Morality and Foreign
Policy.

time and place. Natural laws once discovered can provide universal and immutable guides to action. The
Higher Law undergirding the American Constitutional
system rests on a modern approximation of natural law
as do certain meta codal principles in international
relations such as fair dealing among nations and faith-
ful adherence to international treaties.

The reactions against natural law, however imposing its sacred and secular defenses, are foreshadowed
in the doubts of an ancient thinker such as Cicero.
Such questioning beginning in classical times had grown
in strength by the seventeenth century. Cicero warned:
"It has been observed that the laws of nature were
either too general to offer much help in concrete cases
or too specific to claim universal and absolute authority."[1] Natural law precepts in their application have
not infrequently become the property of the privileged
and the strong, leading the philosopher Pascal to argue
in Pensées, No. 28: "Justice is subject to dispute;
might is easily recognized and is not disputed. So we
cannot give might to justice, because might has gain-
said justice....And thus being unable to make what is
just strong, we have made what is strong just."

Both the classical and the Christian versions of
natural law fell under criticism from modern philosophers and theologians. The critics of the classical
view maintained that the Platonic, Aristotelean and
Stoic outlooks all contributed to substantial misunder-
standings regarding the nature of man by insisting
that man was to be understood primarily from the stand-
point of the uniqueness of his rational faculties.
What is unique in man is his noûs and while this can
be translated as spirit, and for Plato the highest
element of the soul, the primary emphasis has been
on man's capacity for reason and thought. Mind is
sharply distinguished from body. From the time of
Parmenides on, Greek philosophy assumed an identity
between being and reason, on the one hand, and on the
other presupposed that reason works its influence on
unformed and formless matter which resist reason and
is never fully responsive. In Aristotle, matter is
"a remnant non-existent in itself unknowable and alien
to reason, that remains after the process of clarifying
the thing into form and conception."[2] Plato and Aristotle share a common rationalism and along with it a
dualism with only reason being seen as creative principle, immortal and identified with God. Comparing the
classical and Christian versions of natural law,
Reinhold Niebuhr wrote:

While the classical view of human
nature is optimistic when compared
with the Christian view (for it
finds no defect in the center of
human personality) and while it
has perfect confidence in the
virtue of the rational man, it
does not share the confidence of
the moderns in the ability of all
men to be either virtuous or happy.
Thus an air of melancholy hangs over
Greek life which stands in sharpest
contrast to all pervasive optimism
of...bourgeois culture, despite the
assumption of the latter that it had
merely restored the classical world
view....Primarily, it was the brevity
of life and the mortality of man which
tempted the Greeks to melancholy.[3]

Greek tragedy by comparison with Greek philosophy
finds that human life in its effort to be creative
is also destructive and despite the counsel of Greek
philosophers calling for restraint and moderation,
tends to confirm Nietzsche's observation: "Every doer
loves his deed more than it deserves to be loved."[4]
Thus there is no resolution or at most a tragic resolution, between the vitalities of life and the principle
of measure; the various vitalities in life remain permanently in conflict not only with Zeus but with one
another. This profound problem posed so persistently
in Greek tragedy has tended to be largely ignored or
passed over by the group of modern writers who have
revived classical Greek political thought.

2. The Standards of Ethical Theories

The question of standards is by logic and past
practice closely bound up with that of guides to action. The distinction is made, however, in international law and in some branches of political theory
that standards depend for their credibility less on
whether they are universally observed than whether
they provide signposts and pointers to what is right
and just. According to leading jurists, nations weigh
principles of international law in the shaping of foreign policy as they weigh other principles of politics
and economics. Policymakers must decide which principles to follow weighing putative costs and advantages.

The validity of a standard in law or politics does not necessarily depend on its observance. In law, the writings of jurists and publicists help to define a standard as do the common experiences of civilized nations. Positivists and natural law theorists may differ on whether standards are a product primarily of the experience of states or derive from a certain a priori principles, but both appear to accept a similar definition of nature, use and limitations of standards.

To hold to this view is not to argue that the meaning or content of legal and political standards are fixed once and for all and for all time. Paul Freund, Harvard University's great legal scholar has written:

> It is no disparagement of a work of
> art or of its interpreters that it
> takes on new relevance, yields new
> insights, answers to new concerns,
> as the generations pass. Nor is it
> a reproach to a Constitution intended
> to endure for ages to come, and to
> meet the various crises in human
> affairs or to its interpreters that
> it too responds to changing concerns
> of the society to which it ministers."[5]

Freund continues this line of reasoning showing that Hamlet has in successive historical periods been interpreted as a story of revenge, an inquiry into sanity, a study of mother-fixation or an example of the death wish. None of these perspectives are necessarily wrong; each possesses some validity. In the same way, "it need not be a cause of despair that to one generation the Constitution was primarily a means of cementing the Union, to another a safeguard of property, to another a shield of access to political participation and equality before the law."[6] In scholarship, the standard for the historian is objectivity but as Professor Stuart Hughes of Harvard has shown, objectivity "is to be valued only if it is hard-won--only if it is the end result of a desperate and concious battle to rise above partisan passion."[7] Quoting E.H. Carr, an Oxford University historian, "Man's capacity to rise above his social and historical situation seems to be conditioned by the sensitivity with which he recognizes the extent of his involvement in it."[8]

110

Therefore, the interpretation of Hamlet, the Constitution and historical objectivity all involve standards, but standards whose application and expression
are relativized by circumstances. Or in the language
of Professor Freund: "new vistas in constitutional
law are not, in my judgment, boundless...they are not
free of shadows and even treacherous turns."[9] These
turns are made more treacherous, one might add, when
practice departs too far from standards. However, law
and politics in practice resemble art more than science. New vistas open as experience broadens needs
and perspective. "In neither discipline will the
craftsman succeed unless he sees that proportion and
balance are essential, that order and disorder are
both virtues when held in proper tension."[10] The student of law and politics must seek both light and cross-
lights. "There are," Freund concludes in words that
must throw despair into the heart of the sycophant,
"no absolutes in law or art except intelligence."[11]
And intelligence has greater resources than reason,
the student of morality should add.

3. An Alternative View of
Transcendence and
Relativism

The question remains whether the prevailing viewpoints we have explored taken alone or together exhaust
the search for transcendence in political thought. Or
is there another view which does more justice to the
complexities and problems of politics without the furtherance of illusions? Is there another view that
places in perspective the threefold relation of man
with himself, the communities in which he lives and
an overarching moral and political order?

An alternative approach if it can be identified
must be at odds with the classical view on at least two
important aspects of the problem of justice. First,
history demonstrates that the strong may find the
basis for giving help to the weak in a practical morality combining self-interest and compassion. The
Marshall Plan was a judicious blending of magnanimity
and American national interest. Its constituency was
made up both of churchmen and strategic thinkers concerned about Soviet expansion into the power vacuum
created by a morally and materially devastated Europe.
Within the United States, help to minority and dis-
advantaged groups has rested on similar foundations

111

particularly when business leaders concerned for a
stagnating economy have taken the lead to assist the
underprivileged.

Second, the strong find a further basis for help
to the suffering and the deprived at a second level,
that of a transcendent ethic of justice motivated by
love. Within the family, no purely rational basis can
be found for forgiveness and mutual understanding. The
crushing weight of recurrent encroachments of will
upon will by parents upon children, children upon
parents or spouse upon spouse is so continuous, unrelenting and inescapable that the Biblical injunction
"You must forgive seventy times seven" lies beyond all
rational possibility. Yet for men or nations who with
premeditation or not wreak havoc in each other's lives,
no other prescription is prudent or realistic. Official
religion when linked with politics has every bit as
much a need for the law of love, for as Herbert Butter-
filed has written: "The truth is: that a religion,
and particularly a supernatural religion, can be a
very dangerous thing in the world, unless accompanied
by (and rooted in) a super-abundant charity."12

4. Political Reason and Christian Morality

Nowhere is the essential role of charity and compassion as an "impossible possibility" more apparent
than as expressed in the two mediating principles of
justice--freedom and equality. Freedom rests on the
belief in the dignity of man and the never-ending
possibilities of man the creator. However, freedom is
an instrument of justice, not an end in itself, as all
its intemperate uses by the strong to impose their will
on the work plainly attest. Equality as the second
regulative principle of justice is at war with the
facts of the inevitable disparity in individual talents.
However, political history proves the unwillingness of
men in almost every society permanently to accept the
superiority of one group over others or the subordina-
tion of the many by the few solely because of wealth or
position, vocation or personal endowments and ethnic
or regional identity.

Political reason, for its part, has a role to play
in giving content and meaning to freedom and equality.
The great epic periods of political achievement coin-
cide with the merging of religious and rational insights
and their implementation in policies reflecting

political morality. Taken alone, each set of insights
have their limitations. This is true of religion, for
in Butterfield's outspoken judgment:

> It isn't the function of religion
> or the church to solve the problems
> of diplomacy or to tell governments
> how to balance their budgets. Even
> historians, coming long afterwards
> and able to spend years in studying
> a matter, will be baffled by the
> complexity of the forces and the
> multiplicity of the factors that
> happen to underlie a particular
> crisis, and these many people--
> who think they can solve the prob-
> lem, generally turn out to have
> overlooked some particularly
> awkward aspect of the case, and
> ignored some inconvenient consid-
> erations. Real statesmanship, of
> course, requires the ability to
> hold in one's mind a whole jungle
> of relevant details, a whole forest
> of complicating inconsistencies.[13]

This is one side of the equation justifying the
role of political reason, though not of abstract rationalism, in balancing the "enthusiasm" of faith and
religion. In seventeenth century England, Lord
Clarendon warned that ecclesiastical leaders were not
well-suited for governing a country or carrying out
political responsibility. Something more than worthy
motives or noble purposes was needed. Butterfield
goes even further than Charles II's chief minister,
Clarendon, in judging who may be qualified saying: "I
have parallel misgivings about the capacity of academic
people in political affairs; and I seem always to acquire an extra head-ache when I know that another university professor is being called to the White House
or to No. 10 Downing Street."[14]

Yet if religion has its limits as a pathway to
political justice and especially to wise statesmanship,
so too does every form of rationalistic or time-bound
hierarchical thought. It is of course tempting to
argue that freedom and equality would have broken
through in western civilization regardless of the
influence of religious tradition. The Greeks after
all were the architects of much of democratic thought

manifested in the Greek city states. But ideas such as equality were set loose in the early modern world by believers who quoted the Bible, wrote that Christ had made all men free and had faith that all human beings were equal in the sight of God. In eighteenth century England, society included at its lowest stratum "brutalised masses of people" and above them "more innocuous people entirely unfitted for intellectual pursuits--creatures who obeyed their masters like dumb animals" and looked the part. Writing of the changes in English society and history's judgment on these people, Butterfield reports:

> Their betters--the people higher up
> in society, saw (very rightly in
> fact) that there was no hope of
> giving these people the franchise
> and getting them to take part in
> politics; and indeed it was assumed
> that the same would be the case with
> their children and grandchildren--it
> was assumed that their breed was
> basically unfitted for mental pursuits.
> It was John Wesley who, precisely on
> religious grounds, saw the potential-
> ities of these creatures--saw that...
> salvation...was intended for them too,
> and raised them to a higher conscious-
> ness of themselves. The sons of those
> whom he trained to be lay-preachers...
> became important in the development
> of political consciousness in England,
> and we find them among the political
> agitators and trade union leaders of
> a later age.15

Individualism as a modern concept struck roots in this soil threatened through its earliest history by opposing forces. It owed a great deal at the dawn of the modern age to the Christian teaching that man was a creative spirit, "that every single person [was] of superlative value, born for eternity, and therefore incommensurate with anything else in the created uni-verse."16 The force of individualism has declined in mass technological society. Without a fresh injection of the religious doctrine of personality, it isn't clear today how long it will hold its own.

A further question however must be asked. What influence have such religious principles exerted in the history of statecraft? Here the record is less

114

clear and unambiguous. No one can ignore the crimes that were committed in the name of religion in "the Wars of Religion," whether by the followers of Christianity or Islam. Not only did religion introduce a fanaticism that made warfare more cruel but it added substantially to the difficulty of restoring peace. Religion is a matter of ultimate belief but political religions are the inventions of men and are as arbitrary as their will. The business of diplomacy is acommodation, not the resolution of ideological disputes. Historians look back to the sixteenth and seventeenth centuries and see the wars between Protestants and Catholics as more brutal than all wars until those of the twentieth century. Throughout the eighteenth century, as in the period following World Wars I and II, text writers and diplomatists warned that such conflicts must never again occur. The foreign policies put forward by religious people are all too likely to become entangled with patriotic fervor and vested interests are sanctified as though they represented absolute truth. All too often, those who espouse a certain faith subordinate it in practice to some quite limited political end which they invest with all the sanctities of their religious faith.

However, alongside this rather grim and hopeless picture of religious warfare and strife, the historian may discover another more hopeful chapter which is oftentimes overlooked. The Spanish conquest of South America is the story of a religious people who came as conquerors, some of whose leaders claimed the right to enslave the native inhabitants. These conquests led to a historic religious and international law debate. A group of Spanish monks, who have been called the precursors of modern international law, raised the question as to whether Christian principles were being violated in the name of the advance of civilization. In the controversy thus provoked, the religious critics of the Spanish conquest sought to define the human rights of a conquered people. They asked for a statement of what was legitimate treatment of a strange and remote people who refused to accept the truth of Christianity. Put in another frame, what would have been their rights if their conquerors had been Mohammedans who sought to impose the will of Allah? The Spanish writers who posed the issue drew on the Bible, Aristotle, St. Thomas Aquinas and the Common Law, and, depending on their sources, came to rather divergent conclusions. The writers who rested their arguments on Aristotle maintained that the "natives were more like animals...

115

below the use of reason, and Aristotle had said that
those who lacked the use of reason could be legitimately enslaved."[17] An early sixteenth century Pope
offered another argument saying "that God intended all
men for salvation, and that the Indians must be regarded as having the use of reason--a suficient share
of it to understand the Gospel at any rate."[18] An
ancient religious tradition thus provided a concept
of moral and political reason which guided statesmen
to different policies than Greek rationalism.

5. The Cold War and Transcendence

It would be claiming too much for the uses of the
transcendent truths of religion to maintain that its
central concepts are readily translatable in an era of
the Cold War. Religious people are for one thing a
minority voice in the advanced democracies. They have
the same rights and opportunities of persuasion as any
other group--but no more. Their knowledge and profes-
sional skills are usually far behind those of trained
diplomats. "It may seem an odd thing to say, Professor
Butterfield acknowledges, "especially when one is speaking as a Christian, but I think you need somebody
soaked in the whole science of what we call Power Politics to be responsible for the subtle acts of judgment
required."[19] Saints for the most part have not been
especially gifted in the conduct of great power negotiations. The clashes between nation-states are too
bruising and power-laden to lend themselves to the
gentle suasion of religion.

At the same time, too much impatience and anxiety
in foreign policy is often the source of tragic mis-
understanding, miscalculation and error. The Autho-
rized Version of the Old Testament offers one of those
wise maxims which men and nations ignore at their peril:
"Fret not thyself because of evil-doers." Young and
inexperienced democracies are endangered by neglect of
this maxim and certain nations, the Weimar Republic
for example, have been delivered into the hands of a
dictator because of anxiety and doubt generated by
critics within and outside the state. Doesn't the
Biblical counsel lead to self-denial and inaction?
Butterfield thinks not and explains: "It doesn't mean
that you must never try to right a wrong but I think
it explicitly intends to remind you that you must not
expect to win every time, you must say you will make
no peace with Heaven, until all evils are eradicated."[20]

116

Thos who fret themselves too much are likely, through exercising too much impatience and self-righteousness, to bring about a greater evil than those they oppose.

What, then, is the positive contribution of religion to foreign policy beyond its counselling of restraint? Butterfield and Morgenthau have warned it lies outside the realm of any kind of precise guidance in the choice of specific or concrete policies. It can, however, help in providing a proper background of ideas. It can assist men in straightening out notions about human motivations and the persistence of selfishness and sin. It can free men of the belief that all our problems could be solved except for those caused by a handful of criminals whereas "the really knotty problem is that of human nature generally--the moderate cupidities of all men play their part."[21] There are limits even for religion for as Butterfield observes: "Because of the contradictions and paradoxes involved, the realm of international relations, more than any other field, is liable to suffer at one and the same time from the cupidities of the wicked, the fears and anxieties of the strong and the unwisdom of the idealists."[22]

Nowhere is the high price of fretting oneself because of evil doers as great as when very powerful nations stand on the precipice of war. History abounds with examples of terrible wars of mighty nations, each thinking itself in the right, each caught up in the same moral predicament, each believing it had made its share of concessions for peace. Historians looking back after the event to the outbreak of conflict debate the issue of war guilt, revise their viewpoints and try vainly to remember or reconstruct the deeper causes of the struggle. Most often they find that fear was a factor. As in personal relations, so in wars, aggression is often the result of anxieties and fears. The leaders of anxious nations try to dispose of their fears through bold imperialistic threats or deeds. Religion ought to check the rash acts of an anxious sovereign. It offers a chance of helping nations find a way out from a condition of Hobbesian fear of the kind that brought on World War I--a war historians today characterize as an unnecessary war, a war which might have been avoided with even a marginal reduction of national fears. Religionists would advocate that diplomats should strive for the "moral margins" which might break the cycle of fear and of insecurity leading to aggression.

Writing of the Cold War and following this trend
of thought, Butterfield suggests:

> ...perhaps...the most Christian
> thing that could happen would be
> for one of the Great Powers
> (acting not out of weakness
> but out of strength) to risk
> something... involving a trust
> in human nature this time, even
> though we know how foolish it is
> to trust in human nature. Some-
> thing of that sort might be re-
> quired, just as a marginal experi-
> ment...because it happens to be
> the only way out of the worst of
> deadlocks, the tightest of pre-
> dicaments.[23]

Lest this suggestion be considered "soft" or a form of
unconditional surrender, Butterfield quickly adds:
"keep out the sentimentalists [in another place, he
warns against "the parsons"] and those for whom giving
way is easy--they will come forward bringing surrender
to Russia in their outstretched hands."[24] Someone
fairly hard-boiled, a modern Bismarck, would be needed
to execute a policy involving such a risk, Butterfield
insists, but the basis would be one of looking for a
realistic way out of the present impasse from the stand-
point of political prudence and practical morality.
Nations have shown magnanimity in the past, and sometimes a general peace has been restored for a long time,
as in 1815 after the Congress of Vienna, in 1866 thanks
to Bismarck after the defeat of Austria and following
World War II when the United States took the lead in
fashioning more magnanimous arrangements with Germany
and Japan. A spirit of political wisdom and magnanimity may offer the best hope today whether in relations
between Israel's Begin and Egypt's Sadat or Russia's
Brezhnev and the United States' Carter.

This proposal by the distinguished Regius Professor
of History at Cambridge University, who is also a giant
in the field of religious history, illustrates not only
the possibility of an alternative foreign policy for
the Cold War. It also presents in highly concrete terms
a new relationship between transcendent religious truths
and the relativities of contemporary international politics. Its author is modest and tentative in the claims
he makes for such a policy. He asks only that we not

pass judgment too quickly on its prospects. The same needs only to be said in conclusion about the more general alternative framework for thinking about normative foreign policy and politics.

FOOTNOTES

[1] Edmond Cahn, *The Sense of Injustice*. (Bloomington, Indiana: Indiana University Press, 1949), 6.

[2] Werner Jaeger, *Aristotle*. (London, England: Oxford University Press, 1934), 337ff.

[3] Reinhold Niebuhr, *The Nature and Destiny of Man*, Vol. I, *Human Nature*. (New York: Charles Scribner's Sons, 1945), 9.

[4] Frederich Nietzsche, *Kritik und Zukunft der Kultur*, Ch. IV, Par. 13.

[5] Paul A Freund, *On Law and Justice*. (Cambridge, Massachusetts: Harvard University Press, 1968), 8.

[6] *Ibid*.

[7] Stuart Hughes, "Is Contemporary History Real History?" *The American Scholar*, Vol. 32, 1963, 520.

[8] *Ibid*.

[9] Freund, *op. cit.*, 20.

[10] *Ibid*.

[11] *Ibid*.

[12] Sir Herbert Butterfield, unpublished paper on "Religion and Politics," 1.

[13] Butterfield, *op. cit.*, 4.

[14] *Ibid*., 2.

[15] *Ibid*.

[16] _Ibid._, 7.

[17] _Ibid._, 9.

[18] _Ibid._

[19] _Ibid._, 11.

[20] _Ibid._, 11-12.

[21] _Ibid._, 12

[22] _Ibid._

[23] _Ibid._, 10.

[24] _Ibid._

Herbert Butterfield's Writings

1924   The Historical Novel. Cambridge, England:
     The University Press.

1929   The Peace Tactics of Napoleon 1806-1808.
     Cambridge, England: The University Press.

1931a   Select Documents of European History 1715-
     1920. Ed. Herbert Butterfield. New York:
     H. Holt and Co.

1931b   The Whig Interpretation of History. London,
     England: G. Bell.

1939   Napoleon. New York: Duckworth.

1940   The Statecraft of Machiavelli. London,
     England: G. Bell.

1944   The Englishman and His History. Cambridge,
     England: The University Press.

1949a   George III, Lord North, and the People, 1779-
     1786. London, England: G. Bell.

1949b   The Origins of Modern Science. London,
     England: G. Bell.

1949c   Christianity and History. London, England:
     G. Bell.

1951a   Christianity in European History. London,
     England: Oxford University Press.

1951b   History and Human Relations. London, England:
     Collins.

1951c   The Reconstruction of an Historical Episode:
     The History of the Enquiry into the Origins
     of the Seven Years' War. Glasgow, Scotland:
     Jackson.

1953   Christianity, Diplomacy, and War. New York:
     Abingdon-Cokesbury Press.

1955   Man on His Past. Cambridge, England: The
        University Press.

1957   George III and the Historians. London,
        England: Collins.

1960   International Conflict in the Twentieth
        Century: A Christian View. New York:
        Harper.

1966   Diplomatic Investigations: Essays in the
        Theory of International Relations. Ed.
        Herbert Butterfield and Martin Wight.
        Cambridge, Massachusetts: Harvard University
        Press.

1971   On Chinese and World History. With Cho Ysu
        Hsu and William H. McNeil. Hong Kong.

1972   Sincerity and Insincerity in Charles James
        Fox. The British Academy, London, England:
        Oxford University Press.

Books About Butterfield

Geyl, Pieter. *Encounters in History*. London, England:
    Collins, 1963.

God, History, and Historians. Ed. C.T. McIntire.
    New York: Oxford University Press, 1977.

Some Twentieth Century Historians. Ed. S. William
    Halperin. Chicago: University of Chicago
    Press, 1961.